Praise for *Organizing for the Spirit*

"With technology pushing us toward ever-increasing ano-nymity, Sunny Schlenger's *Organizing for the Spirit* is a much-needed antidote. Her new book reflects her insight-ful understanding of human nature, offering narrative and exercises that ring true on every page."

—Jacqueline Hess, senior project director,
Academy for Educational Development

"Sunny's excellent book fits all of us who ever wondered, Why me? Why this stuff? This is a stimulating, out-of-the-box exploration of the internal forces that govern our daily lives. A must-read for anyone who is looking for the elusive key to that all-so-desirable organizational comfort zone."

—Gordon Cucullu, author, speaker, and columnist;
lieutenant colonel, retired, U.S. Army

"Before you buy yet another personal organizer in hopes of finally getting your life in order, you need to get reac-quainted with who you are and what you really want to do. *Organizing for the Spirit* takes you on a journey of self-dis-covery that can help you find more time for what's really important to you."

—Michelle Stanten, senior editor,
Prevention Magazine

"*Organizing for the Spirit* is fabulous! I believe strongly in the importance of this work, especially the premise that everything is connected, including the smallest details of our lives."

—Valerie F   om

"Will help anyone who has struggled with organization to create harmony between their possessions and their lifestyle."

—Lisa Kanarek, author, *Home Office Solutions* and *Organizing Your Home Business*

"Sunny has provided us with a road map for self-knowledge and growth, that is as practical as it is inspirational and personal."

—Stephen C. Garbarini, clinical psychologist

Also by Sunny Schlenger
How to Be Organized in Spite of Yourself

Organizing
for the Spirit

Organizing
for the Spirit

Making the Details of Your Life
Meaningful and Manageable

Sunny Schlenger

Foreword by Harriet Schechter

JOSSEY-BASS
A Wiley Imprint
www.josseybass.com

Published by Jossey-Bass
A Wiley Imprint
989 Market Street, San Francisco, CA 94103-1741   www.josseybass.com

Names have been changed to protect confidentiality.

Jossey-Bass books and products are available through most bookstores. To contact Jossey-Bass directly call our Customer Care Department within the U.S. at 800-956-7739, outside the U.S. at 317-572-3986, or fax 317-572-4002.

Jossey-Bass also publishes its books in a variety of electronic formats. Some content that appears in print may not be available in electronic books.

Library of Congress Cataloging-in-Publication Data
Schlenger, Sunny.
  Organizing for the spirit : making the details of your life meaningful and manageable / Sunny Schlenger; foreword by Harriet Schechter.— 1st ed.
    p. cm.
  ISBN 0-7879-6759-9 (alk. paper)
  1. Self-actualization (Psychology) I. Title.
  BF637.S4S345 2004
  646.7—dc22   2003023202

Printed in the United States of America
FIRST EDITION
PB Printing   10 9 8 7 6 5 4 3 2 1

Contents

Foreword by Harriet Schechter   xi

Acknowledgments   xv

Introduction   1

PART ONE:
Discovering Your True Self   3

Chapter One: Begin at the Beginning   5
Chapter Two: Play Detective   10

Part Two:
Developing Your True Self   27

Chapter Three: Be Who You Are   29
Chapter Four: Be Where You Are   55
Chapter Five: Enjoy Your Life   84
Chapter Six: Give Back   110
Conclusion: The End of One Story   137

The Author   139

To My Dad, Stanley Plaine 1923–2003
My Biggest Fan

Foreword

I think I'd better warn you about something," Sunny Schlenger said. She had just asked me if I'd write the Foreword to her new book, *Organizing for the Spirit*, and I—shamelessly flattered—had immediately agreed to do it. After all, it *is* an honor to be asked to write a Foreword, especially for a book by an author whose work you admire tremendously. Sunny's previous book, *How to Be Organized in Spite of Yourself*, is a classic—one of the best on the topic of getting organized.

Only now she was telling me that there's something shocking in her new book—something I needed to know about before I read it. "Is there nudity?" I joked. But Sunny's tone was dead serious. "I don't know how you're going to take this," she said. Then she dropped the bombshell. "In the book I say. . . *there is no such thing as clutter.*"

No such thing as clutter?! She had to be kidding. Here I am, the author of a book titled *Let Go of Clutter*, and she's saying there's no such thing as . . . Well, Sunny has a great sense of humor, that's all.

But it turned out she wasn't kidding—as you'll see in Chapter One. There it is, top of the page, first thing, in italics: *There is no such thing as clutter.* What blasphemy! You can imagine my outrage and indignation. That is, until I started reading Sunny's wise and wonderful observations about "the stuff of life."

A good book can change the way you think about all sorts of things. *Organizing for the Spirit* does more than that: it will change the way you *feel* about *your* things, the things that are cluttering up your life and making you feel overwhelmed, discouraged, and just plain unhappy. And it may also change the way you feel about yourself. If you have ever felt as though you could never "be organized," this book is exactly what you need to help you discover the organized person within.

Yet *Organizing for the Spirit* is more than an organizing book—it's a guidebook to a new life. Sunny shows how organizing is not an end in itself; it's a means of discovering who you are, and who you can be. In a warm and encouraging voice (it seems as if she is talking directly to you) she shares true stories from her own life and those of her clients to illustrate concepts that are creative, innovative, and motivating. It's like having your very own wise fairy godmother accompany you along your organizing journey, helping you avoid the pitfalls and pratfalls that line the path toward enlightenment.

In the pages that follow, Sunny gently but expertly guides you step by step through the process of uncovering who you are—and who you are meant to be. She makes the work of self-exploration miraculously fun and easy through simple yet effective exercises. Along the way you'll find out how to identify which outgrown dreams and expectations you are ready to jettison, and how to choose what you truly want to replace them with.

Sunny's refreshing candor about her personal struggles with procrastination and how she sometimes falls short of following her own advice, lets you see how you, too, can accept your own mistakes and imperfections with grace and humor. And the inspiring examples from the many interesting people Sunny has learned from will make you want to keep moving forward in a most joyful way.

The writer E. M. Forster once made this observation: "I suggest that the only books that influence us are those for which we are ready, and which have gone a little farther down our particular path than we have yet got ourselves."

I believe you are ready for *Organizing for the Spirit*.

Harriet Schechter
Santa Barbara, California

Acknowledgments

*O*rganizing for the Spirit has been such an amazing journey! What began as a series of weekly e-mail "newsletters" grew into a book through the encouragement of some very special people. Thanks to Anne Chipman-Zipfel, for planting the first seed when she said, "You *are* teaching this stuff, aren't you?"; Olga Silberg for getting me moving on the first newsletter; Harriet Schechter for being a constant source of advice and support on the road to publication; Tana Fleischer and Melanie Hemingway for helping me to see myself as a "real writer"; Betsy Brown for helping to fashion the initial proposal.

All of the subscribers to my Organizing for the Spirit newsletter; the members of my original Organizing for the Spirit support groups—Mary Amoroso, Karel Bodamer, June Byrne, Doreen Conlon, Diane Hyman, Rita Kron, Arlene LoCola, Susan Sarao, and good friends Elayne Blut and Jeannette Moser-Orr, whose collective wisdom and sense of humor kept me from jumping off the roller coaster ride on numerous occasions.

Susan Lang, Debra LoGuercio, and Dot Miller who "always knew"; Helene Miller whose energetic outlook on life is a constant inspiration; and Ellen Daniels, whose talents are exceeded only by her tremendous generosity.

Dave Rubin and Bonnie Berish, the creative partnership at JORB, Inc., who designed and maintained my original website and newsletter archives; Fran Rizzo, Cindy Callaghan, and Marcie Cooper who shared their time and stories; Muriel B. Fielo, Roberta Roesch, and Vera Struble, role models and friends.

My wonderful agent, Natasha Kern, and her assistant Ruth Widemer; equally wonderful editors Julianna Gustafson and her assistant Chandrika Madhavan; the design staff of Paula Goldstein, and my entire Jossey-Bass production and marketing team; my terrific long-time publicist, Andrea Pass.

Finally, gratitude and appreciation to my mom, Thelma Plaine; my brother and sister-in-law, Jeff and Caryn Plaine; my children Lauren and AJ; and of course to my husband, Roy (Gustavson), who makes all things possible.

Sunny Schlenger
Fair Lawn, New Jersey
February 2004

Organizing
for the Spirit

Introduction

I had asked some friends and clients to e-mail me about what the concept of "organizing for the spirit" meant to them. One respondent wrote the following, which goes right to the heart of the question. She said, "To me, organizing for the spirit needs to happen when your life has become so filled that it is overwhelming, particularly emotionally. Life has become too choked up with stuff, and some of the stuff isn't even things you want. It's like a hall closet that's too full to close and things are falling out when you open it.

"So at some point you hit your limit and realize the closet has to be sorted through. You haul everything out and examine each item. And then when you only have the things in your life that really matter and have weeded out all the things that are toxic, your spirit has space to grow. Your 'closet' is organized, and your spirit doesn't get all locked up trying to keep everything from spilling out anymore. You're free."

Organizing for the Spirit is about freedom—the freedom you can attain when you realize that everything in your life is connected. Understanding the connections between what you do, what you've saved, and what you want out of life will start you on an amazing journey of discovery and personal development—through the transformational art of organization.

I've been on this journey for a number of years now, and in the process have managed to become not only more productive but more fulfilled as well. By viewing my time expenditures and space utilization as reflections of my blossoming spirit—my true essence—I've achieved a satisfying sense of wholeness and peace that once seemed beyond my reach.

I invite you to come with me on this journey—to learn how to make practical, everyday decisions that reflect who you really are and who you want to be, and to understand that the simplest choices about how you arrange your life can have a tremendous effect on your spirit's ability to flourish.

Let's open that proverbial closet and, this time, experience the joy and harmony of organizing for the spirit.

PART ONE

Discovering Your True Self

Who lives in your house? Who works in your office? Do you think you really know the individual who occupies your chair? Maybe it's time to take a closer look.

1

Begin at the Beginning

Here's a radical idea for you: *There is no such thing as clutter.* Your belongings carry significance; they are more than just *things* that litter your house or apartment.

And the contents of your to-do list are more than just the items not completed by the end of the day. They're extensions of you—representations of what has had some sort of value in your life. Nothing is separate. Evidence of your personal style, your needs, your idiosyncrasies, your priorities, and your passions surround you. Have you ever thought about what they're saying?

In the twenty-five years that I've been a professional organizer and personal coach, the most frequent (and actually amazing) comment that I hear is this: "You give me permission to be *me!*" In my first book, *How to Be Organized in Spite of Yourself* (NAL Inc., NY 1989; Penguin-Putnam Inc., NY 1999), I identified ten different styles of managing time and space that determine which organizational products and systems are best for each individual. I don't believe that getting organized is simply a matter of solving a series of problems; it's learning how to make personal, individual choices that will bring you closer to who you are and who you'd like to be.

Organizing for the Spirit is about sustaining an environment that supports you and helps balance the demands of everyday living with the pursuit of your dreams. It's about taking care of yourself so you can take care of others, and about understanding how this process contributes to the development of peace and integrity in your everyday life.

CONNECTING TO LIFE'S "STUFF"

So how do you connect to the "stuff" of life in a way that energizes and empowers you, and enables you to live your own life to the fullest? It begins with an analysis of where you are today—an analysis, mind you, not a judgment, because no judgment is being made here. What we're doing is taking inventory of where you are to see if the way you spend your time and energy is the way you *want* to be spending it.

Discovery

We start by playing detective—imagining that *you* don't live in your house and *you* are not the author of your to-do list but that you've been given the assignment of finding out everything you can about the person who does live there and making out that person's list. You'll be taking a tour of each room and determining what the décor says about its owner's style and interests.

And you'll be examining this person's day planner or to-do list to see what she or he is busy doing each day. Are many hours spent in the office? What happens on the week-ends? How about on days off and holidays? Are there appointments to go to the gym? Lunches with friends? Book Club meetings or volunteer activities? How much time is devoted to the care and feeding of others? Is there time blocked off for relaxation or personal interests?

Analysis

After discovery comes analysis. This is where you resume your normal identity and ask yourself these questions: Does what you discovered in your "detective tour" ring true? Is the person who is living in your home today accurately reflected in what was found? Are your current values mirrored by what you see? For example, do your tapes or CDs represent your *current* musical tastes, or are they a nostalgic collection of what you enjoyed years ago? Do you still add to your collections, or are they simply collecting cobwebs in the corner? What about pets? Is their upkeep too much work these days? And how about your reading? Are you staying abreast of the things that interest you, or are your shelves too clogged with titles from other periods of your life? And what about your time expenditures? Are you doing the things you say are important to you?

There is nothing wrong with saving reminders and mementos of pleasant times past, nor is it wrong to devote the majority of your hours to either family or work, *if* that feels right for you now. But if your time or space is primari-ly taken up with items that don't support you in who you are today, your spirit may feel stifled and dusty. It's important to remember that you are a combination of the person you were, the person you are today, and the person you aspire to be in the future. Nothing is as constant as change, and few of us are the people we were five years ago. Our environment and activities should be growing with us, but because of time constraints, work, and family demands, we often don't devote the time we should to staying current with our needs.

This is why we must organize for the spirit. We need to feel at home in our bodies, minds, hearts, and souls. We need to know what makes us happy and synthesize the inward and outward expressions of who we are. And to do this, we have to understand where we are in our lives, that is, what our current obligations, priorities, and preferred lifestyles are.

BEGINNING WITH OURSELVES

Too often, our attempts at organization work backwards. We buy a day planner and bring it home, set it down on the table, and wait for *it* to organize *us*. Or we purchase a book, place it on the shelf, and prepare to somehow become better organized through osmosis. It's a decent effort but ultimately not very practical.

We have to begin at the beginning, with ourselves, asking what our own beliefs and values are. Everything we possess and do is related to these concepts; therefore, if we want the details of our lives to lift us higher, infusing and enriching our spirits, we have to understand the connections.

The purpose of this approach is to keep yourself abreast of *who* you are, *where* you are, how you can *enjoy* your life, and how you can *give something back* (make your personal contribution to the world). I believe that these are the cornerstones of a successful life and that *Organizing for the Spirit* will help you build a strong personal foundation.

Organizing for the Spirit is about achieving harmony between our inner and outer selves. When we're living a life of wholeness and integrity, we instinctively know what's right for us. We know when our energy is healthy and moving and when it's stuck. We know which activities build us up and which drag us down. We know how to share our gifts with those we love and those we want to help.

Let's begin with the first step: discovering who you are today.

2

Play Detective

D o you actually *know* the person who's living in your home today? Are you up-to-date with that person's preferences in clothing, décor, food, music, books, movies? When's the last time you took a really good look around? If it's been a while, now's the time to play detective.

Playing detective is easy and fun, and can be a real eye-opener. Examining your home and your to-do list from an analytical point of view is a valuable exercise. I don't mean "analytical" in the sense of asking, "Do I measure up?" I'm not referring to the neatness or cleanliness of your rooms or to the efficacy of your to-do's but rather the statement your rooms and lists make about what's currently important to you.

For example, does the person who lives in this home seem to like plants? Antiques? Knitting? Tropical fish? Is there a multitude of cooking utensils? Have the magazines and books been opened? Are there collections? Travel souvenirs? Photographs? What can you deduce about this person's musical tastes?

YOUR NOTEBOOK

You will be using a notebook or journal to accompany your reading of *Organizing for the Spirit*. Buy any type that makes you feel good when you look at it, touch it, or smell it. It should be a comfortable companion that will house your discoveries about yourself and enable you to be totally honest about the reality of your life.

Also make sure that you're using a favorite pen to record your observations and answers. Attach the pen to the book if you can, so you're not rummaging about for something to write with. The easier you make the process, the more fun it will be.

✎ *ME Versus NOT ME*

First, open your notebook and divide a page into two columns:

ME   NOT ME

The ME column refers to what you find in your living or work space that "speaks" to you. In other words, does the style of furniture, artwork, and room layout reflect your current taste? How about the knick-knacks? The NOT ME column is for things that are not pleasing to your eye.

Next, take about half an hour to walk around your home or office and jot down, in the appropriate columns, what you see. (For now, leave out the belongings of others who share your space.)

Follow the same procedure for your time expenditures, looking at your to-do list or day planner for the past and present week. Ask yourself whether the items listed represent things you want to do (ME column), as opposed to those that don't mirror your real priorities (NOT ME).

YOUR VALUES INVENTORY

The next step is to take a values inventory to make sure that you're in touch with the values you hold today. Although certain fundamental values may stay constant for you over the years, others may not. For example, at one point in your life it may have been necessary for you to focus on getting ahead in your career. But now you've reached a level where you don't need to put in so many extra hours. You may choose to spend more time with your family and friends; if so, your values have shifted from an emphasis on career development, money, and security to personal relationships.

Or the opposite may be true. I'm working with a client, Bob, who in his fifties is ready to change some long-standing and dominant patterns in his life. His main concern is his inability to get organized, but we've "unpeeled the onion" to the point of discovering that some outgrown assumptions lie beneath his problems. It seems that Bob's definition of who he is and what's important to him hasn't been updated in a while. He's operating on old assumptions, and these are now holding him back.

When was the last time you updated your internal résumé? Are the issues that influenced your decisions in the past still controlling your outlook? Are the pressures (imagined or real) that strong-armed you back then continuing to hold you hostage? What are your "truths" today?

Bob was surprised to recognize that certain career sacrifices he had chosen to make years ago, based on family priorities at the time, are no longer required of him. His son is now older and more independent, and this realization frees him to look at his current job status differently and to set some goals that were previously beyond his reach.

I suggested to Bob that instead of starting with an outline of all of the organizational problems he'd like to fix, we begin by investigating where he'd find himself if or when he became as organized as he said he'd like to be. If he wasn't busy looking for things he'd misplaced and racing to meet deadlines as a result of procrastination, what would he be doing?

That question gave him pause. Learning how to manage his disorganization would give him the time he said he wanted to devote to creative analysis; it would allow him to accomplish more, achieve more, and raise his profile within the company. But is that what he really wants to do?

After some intense self-analysis, he's come to the conclusion that, yes, he's ready to take on new challenges, even though that means he'll have to develop additional skills. But having the knowledge of where he wants to go, based on his current values, is allowing him to experience a new level of excitement and anticipation, and that level is fueling the energy needed to tackle change.

✎ *My Values*

What do you value most today?

From the following list of values, select the ten that are most important to you today and write them in your notebook:

Adventure	Challenge	Competence
Affection	Change	Contribution
Autonomy	Community	Creativity

Effectiveness	Job Tranquility	Public Service
Efficiency	Leadership	Recognition
Environment	Location	Religion
Equality	Mature Love	Reputation
Excellence	Meaningful	Security
Excitement	Work	Self-Respect
Expertise	Money	Serenity
Fame	Peace	Spiritual
Family	Personal	Well-Being
Friendship	Growth	Stability
Happiness	Pleasure	Status
Health	Power and	Teamwork
Independence	Authority	Wisdom
Integrity	Privacy	

Once you have identified your top ten values, narrow them down to five.

Of the remaining five, eliminate one at a time until you are left with only one. The one remaining is the strongest of all your fundamental, core values.

ANALYSIS OF THE RESULTS

Now it's time to compare your findings. Are your core values reflected in what you found when you played detective? Does Person A match Person B?

In my own self-analysis, the value of Integrity ranks at the top, just after Family and Friends. Living with integrity is a lifelong quest to honor who we are through both words and actions. So often, we agree to do things we shouldn't, and that, in turn, takes time away from doing the things we should. Living with integrity means being absolutely clear on what we value and using every possible choice point as an opportunity to demonstrate those values.

If, for instance, you determine that your top three personal values are Family, Community, and Self-Respect, then your time expenditures should be more heavily weighted in these areas. If that's not the case and you're doing other things, you need to find out why and what you can do about it. There's no right or wrong when it comes to ranking values; at different times in your life you may feel more strongly about one area than another. What's critical is to be truthful about your priorities and make sure that you walk your talk.

A Total Disconnect

When my client, Mindy, analyzed her daily calendar using the "ME Versus NOT ME" lists, she discovered that her current schedule bore little resemblance to the kind of days she yearned for. First, here's how her day goes now:

Typical Day

4:30 A.M.: Get one of the kids up for morning swim practice, then go back to bed till 7:00 A.M.

7:00 A.M.: Get up again, unload the dishwasher, feed the dogs, get one of the kids up and make breakfast. Head out the door by 7:30 if I'm taking one of them to school, otherwise by 7:50 to get to the office.

8:15 A.M.: Usually am at the office by now, getting a Diet Coke and starting the day.

8:30 A.M.–Noon: Deal with clients and put job tickets through.

Noon: Either go swim with my Master's Swim Group or head to the gym to work out, then grab a bite to eat and head back to the office.

1:30–5:30 P.M.: More dealing with clients, checking on jobs in progress, etc. . . .

5:30 P.M.: Leave work and sit in rush hour traffic for 30 minutes to make my way home.

6:00 P.M.: Generally swing by on my way home and pick up one of the kids at the pool. If husband is working late, then I'm trying to get dinner ready quickly since everyone is starving.

7:30 P.M.: Finished with dinner; the kids go off to do homework. I clean up the dishes, get the vitamins out for the next morning, make school lunches for the next day.

8:00 or 8:30 P.M.: Check e-mail; if time, do BLOG entry. Do laundry or iron if necessary.

9:30 P.M.: Let the dogs out and if lucky go to bed.

And here's a day she'd *really* enjoy:

Ideal Day

7:00 A.M.: Get up to get the kids off to school; drive them there, then come home.

8:30 A.M.: Check e-mail; organize my day. Glad I don't have to go in to an office.

8:45 A.M.: Do freelance writing work or anything else I've got going on that interests me.

11:40 A.M.: Leave to go swim or work out.

1:00 P.M.: Hit the grocery store and run any other errands as necessary.

3:00 P.M.: Have an hour doing something for myself: reading, working in the yard; walking the dogs.

4:00 P.M.: Do some more work: writing, marketing my new projects.

5:15 P.M.: Make dinner and talk about the day with my family.

7:30 P.M.: Finish up any work I may have, or relax and read, or watch TV with the kids.

10:30–11:00 P.M.: Go to bed.

After doing her values analysis, Mindy realized that it was necessary for her to take a financial risk and leave her full-time job in order to create time for her greatest current priorities: her children and her writing. She was fortunate that her husband had a reasonable amount of job security, but she knew that without her additional steady income, they would have to do without a number of extras. Still, the choice was clear. "I don't want to look back on my life and discover that I didn't do the things that make life meaningful for me."

A Good Match

An example of a person making a good match between values and time and space deployment is my friend, Meg. I interviewed Meg for this book because I've always marveled at her eclectic tastes and sense of whimsy. She comfortably mixes items associated with Bob Dylan, Paul Cézanne, Clark Gable, Jerry Garcia, and Albert Einstein all over the walls and tabletops in her house, along with a homemade salt-and-pepper-shaker chess set, a Haitian-art-inspired beaded chest, a glass lamp base filled with concert tickets, and a quilt made from her son's outgrown jeans. I asked Meg to take me on a tour of her home so I could better understand how her decorating scheme reflects her interests and passions, her beliefs and dreams.

As we walked around, I could see that Meg values a number of different things, chief among them her children. Photos of her two sons and a daughter can be found in every room of the house, starting with her office-den where she spends a considerable amount of time. There are large black-and-white portraits and colorful picture cubes, interspersed with the kids' artwork.

"Everything in my house has meaning," she told me. "Every room has its own color and feeling. For example, I work hard in my office, and I want the décor to make me feel good—peaceful and at rest. But I also want to be surrounded by inspiration." Toward that end, she has a framed, blown-up picture of Sedona, Arizona—a memory of a magical trip—hanging next to her desk, along with an enlargement of the words on a small stamp ("Where there is NEED I will provide care; Where there is CARE it is given in love; Where there is LOVE we are given hope; Where there is HOPE we will answer the need.") that remind her of the larger purpose behind her business. (Meg is the executive director of a geriatric assistance agency.)

Whenever possible, she puts herself in the picture so she can remember, intensely and viscerally, what it's like to be in a beautiful spot: in Paris, San Francisco, New York. She blends the old with the new to create an easy flow between time and space, memories and motivation. And the result is a thoroughly enchanting environment.

"The individual rooms reflect my growth and tastes. The backgrounds are all neutral so that I can move things around. And everything is recycled. My best finds have been in people's curbside trash. I can't just go out and buy a lamp that matches the color scheme. It has to have personality."

The steps to the upstairs bedrooms are painted with the letters of her children's favorite bedtime book, *Goodnight, Moon*. Meg's bed is an old metal frame that has been refinished to a violet, pearlized luster. It is surrounded by memorabilia from her late grandmother, a woman she regards as one of her heroes and role models.

"You can tell who I am by looking at what I surround myself with," Meg states simply. "I realize that you have to be brave to take some of the decorating risks that I've taken, such as putting cow spot decals on a brand new refrigerator, but in the final analysis this place is my sanctuary. I need to laugh, and I need to look forward to what life has to offer. That's why over my kitchen sink I have a postcard of an old Airstream motor home. It reminds me that all I really need is a simple life with just a few of the things that are most important to me."

WHEN OLD DREAMS CHANGE

Often, we grow and change without having a clue that Person A no longer matches Person B, that is, what we used to think we want is no longer what we want.

A member of one Organizing for the Spirit group told us of a discovery she had recently made along these lines. She had been chatting with an old friend, who mentioned that he was selling his house. Laurel had always loved his home and for years had hoped that one day she could live there, should he decide to move on. She went to bed that night enthused about the possibility of having this dream come true, only to find that she couldn't sleep. And the reason wasn't excitement. It was confusion.

But why should she be confused? Wasn't this what she had always wanted? The house was perfect; no work needed to be done. Where were her doubts suddenly coming from? It took her all night to understand that this long-term dream of hers was actually an old dream. In the interim, she had remarried and was happily settled with her new husband. Although her dream house was lovely, it wasn't much bigger than the one she was living in. Yes, it would be easy to move forward the way she had always imagined, but was this what she still wanted?

It's reasonable to assume that as we change, our dreams for ourselves will change. But as Laurel's story shows us, we're often not aware that we *are* changing. We may be hanging on to outmoded ideas of what will bring us joy.

How do you know if your dream is an old one? It's not something you can find out intellectually. You have to go within and ask yourself, "How does this feel?" If you're not sure or if you're confused, as Laurel was, you're telling yourself something right then and there. Clarity is one of the hallmarks of living with a dream that's right for you now. A sense of peace is another. There's a difference between having questions about pursuing a certain course of action and having doubts. Questions mean you need more information, whereas doubts imply a level of discomfort that needs to be explored further.

Laurel's experience was meaningful to her because it drove home the awareness of just how much her life had changed. She can release the old dream the same way she releases whatever doesn't fit her life today. She trusts that her next dream house will eventually appear to her, and in the meantime she's very happy to enjoy what she has.

FOLLOW-UP EVALUATION

How much of what you find in the course of making your analysis still makes you feel good when you look at it? Do you still enjoy the artwork on your walls? How about your framed photographs? Are some of them recent? Are the photo subjects still the most important people in your life? Where are your favorite books? Can you find them? What about the kitchen? Are you using the appliances that cover your countertop? Could you use more space or fewer appliances?

It's so very important to ask these questions because we're not just discussing decorating options here. The fact is, it's hard to determine *where* something should go if you don't yet know *whether* it should go anywhere at all. The decisions you make about your kitchen appliances are actually decisions you're making about yourself and what you value—what you're allowing to consume the minutes and hours, square feet, and square yardage of your home.

The phrase "Papers R Us" hints at another way to look around you and evaluate what you see. Because everything, your paper included, is an extension of you, those papers scattered around on table tops or piled in stacks on your desk are making a statement. (This is not about neatness, by the way. Messy papers primarily indicate postponed decisions.) So what statement is your paper making about you? What are you keeping and why? As with everything else in your life, saved papers should be contributing to your well-being, not distracting you from it.

ORGANIZING AS SELF-DISCOVERY

I was sitting across the desk from my client as he sorted through a messy stack of miscellaneous *stuff*. Contained in that pile were items as varied as ATM receipts, a magnifying glass, sale circulars, business correspondence, and a talking postcard.

Suddenly, he held up a fistful of file folders and said, almost defiantly, "These aren't just papers; this is the book I'm writing!" And I smiled and said, "Exactly."

My client had called me in because he was ready to get serious about the book he had been planning to write for years and believed that his chronic state of disorganization was getting in the way. It's true that he had Post-Its with book notes written on them, and envelopes with book notes written on them, and legal pads with book notes written on them all over the place. But that wasn't his biggest problem. The real obstacle was that his energy was scattered all over the place, along with his notes.

As we worked our way through the piles, I noticed that every time he came across a book-related scrap, he actually sat up straighter. He brightened and his voice became stronger. He looked and acted more focused. Now, it just so happened that he had a second desk in the room, so I suggested that we dedicate that space solely to The Book, and as the pile on that desk grew, I actually witnessed the renourishing of a spirit.

And this is not an unusual occurrence. When clients can connect with whatever supports, encourages, or inspires them, I see a transformation. What previously has been a very mundane chore becomes a means of discovery and growth.

That's not to say that digging through years of backlogged magazines is inherently thrilling. But if you whittle the collection down to a manageable size and set aside a small amount of time to page through the interesting ones, you might be able to reconnect with the part of you that is excited by the idea of trying out a gourmet recipe, planting some vegetables, visiting a local gym, or joining a book club.

Or, in cleaning out old file drawers, you might unearth ideas for craft projects, family trips, or new hobbies worth investigating. I've worked with people who pulled out folders full of phone numbers and addresses that they'd forgotten they had, which enabled them to revive old relationships. And one person discovered pages and pages of printed cartoons and jokes and funny stories that she was able to share with a relative who needed cheering up.

Junk drawers, old binders, closet shelves, and ancient Rolodexes can contain hidden treasures, if you're inclined to think along those lines. It all depends on the attitude with which you approach the job of going through them. You don't want to tackle too much at a time, and you have to be careful not to get caught up in self-recrimination if your pack-rat behavior seems to have gotten out of hand. Just view the task as an archeological excavation and see what turns up.

An added benefit is that you can get rid of what you no longer have use for, which frees up all sorts of space for the things you want to surround yourself with today. But the biggest bang for the buck is the surge of energy that comes from pulling yourself back together, in a very literal way.

The very act of gathering similar items in one place can have an amazingly positive effect. Maybe it's the fact that you can actually *see* what you have or the sense of control that accompanies knowing where things are. But the boost is real and the pleasure genuine. You don't have to be a Felix Unger to appreciate the value of organization; all it takes is the experience of connecting with yourself again to realize what's in it for you.

My client still has a lot of piles to go through, and it will be a while before all of those book notes turn up. But the light at the end of the tunnel is definitely there. Most significantly, he can see the direct link between taking the time to plow through papers and putting them where they're supposed to go, and accomplishing what is important to him at this point in his life. He understands that organizing is more than an end in itself; it's a means of discovering who he is and who he can be.

The next step is to develop the foundation—being who you are, being where you are, enjoying your life, giving back—that will underlie your decisions about the best ways to manage your time and space.

PART TWO

Developing Your True Self

If the results of your analysis (comparing what you found when you played detective with what's in your values inventory) did not reveal a satisfying match, this is where you begin to make changes.

We need to feel at home in our minds, our spirits, and our bodies. Our environment and our to-do's should be outward expressions of who we are and what makes us happy:

- Being who we are
- Being where we are
- Enjoying our life
- Giving back something

3

Be Who You Are

There's only one you. Your individuality should be driving everything you do. But sad to say, many of us end up being someone other than who we really are. Whether we haven't discovered our uniqueness yet or we're trying to please someone else (alive or dead), we're not living as authentically as we could. We're settling for lives that are absent the challenges and contributions that rightfully belong to us. We need to learn to live with integrity, be comfortable with our authenticity, and rediscover our personal passions before we can truly be who we are.

Baruch Spinoza said, "To be who we are, and to become what we are capable of becoming is the only end in life." But what, exactly, does it mean to be who we are? One place to begin answering this question is to observe your personal style, not just your style of dressing or decorating or entertaining but everything you do. Personal style is the outward manifestation of your inner self. It showcases your natural preferences and expresses what you truly love.

WHAT ARE YOUR STRENGTHS?

How do we discover who we are? Writing a personal advertisement is one way to begin. Have you ever had the occasion to write a personal ad, like the ones that appear in singles' magazines or in the Personals section at the back of the newspaper? The goal is to catch a potential mate's interest by presenting yourself as attractively as possible, sometimes stretching the truth as far as it will go, or even beyond.

What if you were asked to write an ad that wasn't designed to hook someone but was simply an honest accounting of your attributes or strengths?

Let's try it.

✎ *Ten Positives About Me*
In your notebook, list ten positives about yourself.

This may sound like a very easy assignment, but you'd be surprised at how many people in my workshops have trouble coming up with ten positives. What usually happens is that we tentatively begin to name our strengths, talents, abilities, and outstanding qualities, only to discover that the act of identifying them brings out the voice of our very judgmental Inner Critic: "What do you mean you're *intelligent?* Compared to whom? You know you're not as smart as your cousin Ferdinand! What are you thinking, then, to call yourself intelligent?"

The Critic doesn't stop there. "And you say you're *sensitive?* Yeah, you're sensitive all right—you're *too* sensitive! You let everyone else's problems affect you. And you call yourself a good parent? What about the time you weren't keeping an eye on little Joanna and she got down on the floor and ate the dog's food? And the time you forgot to do ABC, and XYZ happened, and then . . . ."

Our Inner Critic can be a very powerful presence, especially if we haven't identified the Critic's voice. Generally, our Inner Critic is somebody from our past who diminished us in some way and whose opinions we have come to regard as truth. Or our Critic may personify our own perfectionism, which keeps us from enjoying our accomplishments because they don't seem good enough.

An Inner Critic can serve a positive purpose when the voice encourages us to stay on our toes and evaluate our performance in a constructive way. But all too often, we allow it to squash the feelings of pleasure we're entitled to for having put forth our best efforts.

How do you know if you're letting your Inner Critic have a disproportionate say-so? Let's say that you're able to identify only five positives for your personal ad. You go to a few trusted friends and ask them for help in coming up with an additional five. They give you a big smile and start listing. But you find yourself mentally putting your hands over your ears after the first two and protesting, "No, no, no! That can't be right; you must be talking about someone else! Stop. You're making me feel uncomfortable!"

Bingo. Your Inner Critic is running the show. First of all, your friends are not automatically deluded if they compliment you on some facet of your being that you don't agree with. And contradicting them or arguing is actually an insult; you're telling them that their perceptions are wrong. If you have to question those perceptions, it's fairer to ask for examples so you can judge for yourself rather than condemn them outright.

Your role here should be the opposite of what you're automatically inclined to do. You should listen intently so that you can learn something about yourself that you may not have known. And the proper response to what you hear would be just to say thank you. If your friend tells you that you are beautiful, your first reaction might be to think, "She doesn't know what she's talking about." That's your Inner Critic comparing you to your ideal or to others that you or society have deemed beautiful. However, your friend might see you as beautiful because of your smile, your eyes, your kindness or generosity, your sweetness or energy. We all have different ideas of what "beauty" means, and it's worthwhile to question your negative knee-jerk reaction to such a compliment.

The fact is, virtually all of us have many more positive qualities than we can see with our own eyes. Our Inner Critic is merely a reflection of all the negativity we may be used to experiencing and is not the whole truth or final word on our character or personality. We can only put forth our strongest and best selves if we truly believe that they exist, and sometimes we need to trust the positive feedback from those who see what we don't.

Keep doing the "Ten Positives About Me" exercise until you have no trouble listing ten or more positives—and believing them. Remember, your positive qualities are just as real and important as any others, and accepting and building on them will make meaningful growth possible.

LIVING WITH INTEGRITY

Integrity is the state of being whole or entire. As I grow older and become more aware of what's important to me, the more conscious I am of those times when my behavior doesn't reflect my beliefs, that is, when my outside doesn't match my inside and I'm *not* living with integrity.

It used to be that I would ignore those discrepancies and just chalk them up to a desire for expediency—doing things a certain way because it's easier or faster to do them that way. For example, I know that I'm helping my children to mature when I have expectations of them that match their ages and skill levels. If they're supposed to clean up after themselves at mealtime, for instance, but I do it for them because it's too much trouble to chase them down and listen to excuses, I may avoid the discomfort of conflict, but I'm not doing what I know is the right thing to do.

There are times when it's just a lot more comfortable to go for the quick fix and not think about repercussions. But what am I teaching my kids when we don't follow through on our agreements? They're learning that it's OK not to do what you say you're going to do. (By the way, I'm not talking about those times when people have legitimate reasons to beg off. I'm referring to those everyday occurrences when we give in because it's simpler to do that.)

Sometimes we're just too doggoned tired or over- whelmed or irritable or rushed to do what we know is cor- rect. But the question is: Does that make it right? If your goal is to live with integrity, you need to examine this question and figure out what it means to you. Living with integrity is a lifelong quest to honor who you are through your words *and* your actions.

Do you know how to tell what's really important to people? Don't just listen to what they're saying; watch what they do. If someone insists that he believes in healthy living but makes little effort to care for himself properly, what should you think? If someone says that she values family closeness above all else but is hardly ever at home, how significant can that need be? Again, I know that there are times when people have trouble accomplishing what they want to because of factors beyond their control, but I'm not addressing that issue. I'm speaking of the "inner knowing" we have when we don't even try to do what we know we're capable of doing.

Living with integrity means that you face off every day against the million and one excuses that make life easier and that you're honest with yourself about the ways in which you make choices and decisions. And being honest with yourself can be difficult to do, because taking a deep look inside can give you more information than you're prepared to deal with at present. But it's the only place to start if you want to feel as good about yourself as you can.

Living with integrity means that we know when to say yes and when to say no and that we strive to do that, to the best of our abilities.

I've mentioned elsewhere that we often agree to do things we shouldn't, taking time away from things we should do. "Getting it right" involves being absolutely clear on what we value and using every possible choice point as an opportunity to demonstrate those values.

Living a life of integrity always represents a moment-to-moment choice. It's never to late to begin—or to begin again.

BEING AUTHENTIC

One evening, I went to Barnes & Noble to see one of my favorite authors, Anne Lamott. Anne wrote the very popular *Bird by Bird,* a personal primer on the art and craft of writing.

She had just arrived in New Jersey from California and admitted to being quite jet-lagged. She read two passages from her most recent book and then, while hunting for a third, started to laugh at herself and said that she probably ought to be embarrassed at not being able to find her way around her own book, but she wasn't. Nor did she seem to care that she was dressed in old, comfortable jeans and wearing no makeup. She was just pleased to be there with us, sharing her passions.

And I thought to myself, "Wow. This could be me—sharing myself with dozens of strangers who love what I write and not giving a gosh-darn about how I look or sound!" Oops. Hold it right there. That could be me, if only I were as confident and self-assured as Anne Lamott.

There's the rub. Anne says, and I agree, that good writing is telling the truth. That's why we respond the way we do to raw honesty when we hear it. We're starving for that in this age of political spin and polish. But truth and honesty extend beyond the written word; they're a total package, especially when you experience the power of someone being true to herself.

That's precisely what we got with Anne Lamott that night—the whole deal. And the audience loved it because it was so authentic. She wasn't performing for anyone else's benefit; she was just *being*. And that's what I aspire to. I want to be able to just walk out there—calm, relaxed, casual, not worried about my appearance or professionalism—ready to share whatever wisdom I've acquired with people who appreciate my efforts and accomplishments.

But then, in my mind's eye, I see my mother in the first row. I notice that she's tapping her front tooth and nodding at me. I wonder, Do I have a piece of food caught there? Then she makes a sweeping motion over her head, and without thinking I brush back the piece of hair that's fallen forward. I continue to watch her, alert for any other faux pas I need to fix. Is my lipstick smeared? Are my glasses on straight? Buttons all buttoned up?

To be fair to my mother, this is not really about her. In this scenario, she is merely the personification of my perfectionism—my Inner Critic who sits up front and watches and comments on the acceptability of everything I do. And you know what? I'm getting tired of hauling my personal Inner Critic around.

So how do I decide that I'm OK enough to be *me* in public? How does a lifelong people-pleaser go about primarily pleasing just herself? The answer, I believe, can be found in watching people like Anne Lamott.

Anne Lamott clearly enjoys being Anne Lamott. She's at home in her own skin, and that kind of pleasure transmits instantly to an audience. It's not about her kinky, dread-locked blonde hair, her black-rimmed glasses, or her Snapple bottle full of watered-down cranberry juice. It is about her easy laughter and her attempt to pack each breath with as many stories as possible. She's connected to the people who come to hear her, and you can see that connection in her every glance around the room.

Actually, she put her finger on exactly what accounts for her popularity: she's found her voice. Each and every one of us has a distinctive voice, one that most effectively puts forth the truth of the world as we see it. Identifying that voice and having the courage to speak up is all we need to do in order to claim our rightful place. It's about seeking expression, not about seeking approval.

In other words, you're not in a contest. Unless you happen to be in a formal competition of some sort, you're not going up against anyone other than your best self. So the only thing that makes sense is to figure out who you are and be as much of that person as you possibly can be. And if that person happens to have spinach in her teeth and mussed hair that night, so be it.

Sharing Yourself

There are certain seasons of the year when I'm best able to play social catch-up. I find myself looking to renew contact with local people I haven't seen in a while and figuring out how to schedule coffees or teas or even a whole meal with them.

Two friends I managed to get together with recently are both women in their upper seventies. I think about them often, but our lives don't intersect very much, and therefore months can go by before we make a real date to meet. But meet we did. First I met Violet at a bookstore, then Rosa over lunch at a local café.

I've always admired Violet and Rosa; they're both strong, independent women with very definite views on the world. But they're still wonderfully open-minded and very much concerned with staying positive and happy and healthy in a society that does not always treat the elderly kindly.

Violet and Rosa are role models for me, as are my parents, for how to age gracefully while maintaining considerable wit and candor. While many of their contemporaries are consumed with personal ailments, they refuse to focus on the half-empty glass. They consider the process of living to still be in full swing, even if some accommodations have to be made. Their minds remain young and active, and this orientation, combined with the wisdom of their years, gives them an amazing vantage point from which to experience life.

Violet and I sat at our tiny table at the bookstore, trying to balance a hazelnut latte, Earl Grey tea, a cranberry scone, and two lopsided piles of books. She began telling me about the mini-courses that she was taking at the local community college that semester, and my reaction to one course in particular made us both laugh: "It's a course on Ethics," she said, "taught by a wonderful professor whom I had last year. But you have to be over fifty to take it."

"Gee, that's too bad," I replied. "It sounds great!" She looked at me quizzically, and it was only then that I remembered that I *am* over fifty.

We reminisced about the various desserts and discussions we've had at her house and how much I love the atmosphere of her Old World living room. We talked about the times she has reluctantly asked me to drive her to doctors' appointments and to car repair shops after dark. "It's hard surrendering your freedoms as you get older, but that's reality and you do what you must. The trick is to do it with dignity."

Frankly, it hurts to watch her battle cataracts and diabetes and blood pressure problems. As it's difficult to hear about my father's angina and my mom's back pain. It's not that they complain. It's just what is.

But I'm learning so much by watching and listening. I'm increasing my awareness of time and its passage—what it can do to the human spirit and what we can sometimes prevent it from doing. Sharing ourselves—our hours, our energy, our expressions of interest—are the biggest gifts we can give one another. And those gifts become even larger in their significance as we get older.

My friend Rosa and I had our lunch at the café and talked nonstop for two hours. We share a love of writing and of living a life that has many positive things to write about. She was enthusiastic on the subject of all of the music concerts she's been attending, especially her recent choir concert. "We sang some rock music," she told me, "and I was amazed at how little I knew about the history of rock."

"That must have been fascinating," I replied. "Can you tell me some of the songs you sang or the groups they were from?" She looked at me blankly, and we simultaneously burst out laughing. "Yet another senior moment!"

Rosa and Violet are wonderful examples of people being wholly who they are, despite what others may regard as limitations.

We only have so many years on earth to share our whole-ness with each other. Make a date with your favorite older person and let that person know how much he or she is admired and appreciated. You will feel marvelous.

Igniting Your Spark

But what if you're truly stuck when it comes to figuring out your "who-ness"? What if you've been too tired, distracted, busy, or stressed out to be in touch with your authenticity?

I was invited to host an on-line chat for women seeking to experience more happiness in their lives. It was a warm and wonderful session, as it always is for me when people have the courage to step up to the plate and reveal them-selves with all their doubts and uncertainties. It gives us a chance to analyze their stance and take some good practice swings together.

One woman began by saying that she thought she need-ed advice on scheduling her time better because she was never getting to the bottom of her to-do list. But as we chat-ted, it became apparent that, as in most cases, there was a good deal more to her story. In fact, her problem had less to do with *accomplishing* to-do's than it did with *understand-ing* why the to-do's were there in the first place. She was operating as a "human doing" rather than a "human being."

Very often, when we're functioning on automatic pilot, it's because we've lost sight of the motives behind our move-ment. We're doing things by rote and not experiencing the satisfaction we once did. And although improving our sys-tems of time management may allow us to get more done, what's the point if we're not doing the right things?

So, how do you know what's right? The first thing to do is to check in with your body and ask yourself, "How do I feel on those days when I've managed to rest, eat, and exercise properly? Am I still tired? Frustrated? Discouraged? Sad? Although there may be many reasons for having these feelings, one big one is not being in touch with who you are today.

There can be many different ways to define yourself, but they're not meaningful unless they're current. We forget that time really does march on and change is inevitable, and therefore we can't automatically assume that what has made us feel fulfilled in the past is forever going to remain the same.

What typically happens is that we first experience a vague kind of disquiet, which we may try to ignore. And that's when we really start to get uncomfortable, because the subconscious part of us that cares so much about our well-being will step up its efforts to bring the dissatisfaction to our attention. But if we stay too busy to notice, or it's too inconvenient to do something about it, we'll just continue to stuff down our feelings and keep on truckin'. Beneath the surface, though, we do know that we're unhappy, and we can gradually sink into a pit of sadness and despair where we feel too hopeless or helpless to make a change.

It's difficult to be excited about anything when you're feeling down, but that could very well be where your salvation lies. You need to discover (or rediscover) your spark. I believe that spark is never extinguished; rather, it continues to burn quietly like the pilot light in a gas stove. The flame may be low or hidden from your view, but it's definitely there. And I could see it so clearly in the woman I was chatting with.

I asked her what she did that gave her pleasure, and she answered that she loved creating pretty things. But "creating pretty things" was not on her to-do list. And why not? Because her list was already filled with responsibilities and obligations to other people, and there just wasn't enough time or energy to create pretty things for herself.

Does this sound familiar? Has your spark dwindled down to a flicker? If so, it's essential to turn up the heat. Getting in touch with what you love today is the first step. Ask yourself, "If I were asked to share what it is that makes me smile, what would I say? What makes me laugh? What makes my eyes light up and my heart feel full?" The energy generated by these answers is the fuel for your fire and an indispensable part of a truly effective to-do list.

In order to make the best decisions about your life—whether to change jobs, begin a new career, go back to school, get married, have children, relocate, volunteer for something—you have to check in with your internal flame.

No one but you knows what feels exactly right, that is, when it's OK to compromise and when it's not. The goal is to recharge that spark and have it burn so brightly that others see your light and can share in its glow. Your special talents and interests are the beacons that point the way, so make it a point to rediscover yours.

✎ What Makes Me Happy

Turn to a fresh page in your notebook and set a timer for twenty minutes. During that time, list as many things as you can that give

42

you pleasure. The items can range from the smallest of actions, such as scratching your dog behind the ears, to the largest, such as taking a worldwide cruise or climbing a mountain. Try to reach one hundred items.

Then determine how much time each item would take to do. Scratching the dog might be thirty seconds; traversing the globe might be six months or more. Most items will fall somewhere in the middle—between a minute and a day.

This exercise can be quite valuable when figuring out how to fit small pleasures into your day or week. Knowing what you love to do and how much time each activity takes will enable you to give yourself a simple smile or a big boost whenever necessary.

✎ Something Wonderful

This exercise is a particular favorite in my Organizing for the Spirit groups. As a homework assignment, I ask the members to bring in "something wonderful" for the next meeting—a treasure that has personal value. That's your assignment, too. Find a personal touchstone or keepsake and identify for yourself what makes it wonderful.

Many of the wonderful things brought into our workshops have had to do with a special relationship with family, friends, or pets. They've ranged from a collection of valor medals from World War II, to a tiny china cup and saucer, to a picture of a very happy puppy. Photographs are probably the most frequently shared items because they capture most succinctly the essence of that special relationship. But my

43

favorites are the most visceral—the things that make a person *feel* the sense of wonderfulness.

Once a group member brought in an audiotape of a band and chorus belting out, "When the Saints Come Marching In," recorded at a giant choral gathering of over seventeen hundred people. And the bag of brightly colored breakfast cereal that a nursery school teacher's aide showed us, with the explanation that she found it "fun to go home and try what the kids do because it always looks interesting." Then there was the basket of rhubarb picked from a grandmother's garden, a handful of red Georgia clay from a terrific getaway weekend, a wooden fish, an artificial orchid, a beach plum from Cape Cod.

There are no criteria for what makes a thing wonderful, but it does tell you a lot about what's important to someone. I love watching people's faces when they talk about what makes their treasure special. My teenage son told me that if he were in my group he would bring in our dog, and the softness in his expression when he said that was something I don't get to see very often. The woman who brought in the cup and saucer shared, quietly, the lovely memories of afternoon tea with an elderly neighbor who has since passed on. I've seen pride, affection, tears, and laughter, but mostly *appreciation* of people and places that we may not stop to think about very often but who may have a profound impact on who we are today.

Collecting Your Thoughts

Making lists of favorite things is another way to tap into what makes you, you. Lists of favorite books, songs, movies, food, animals, and personal heroes will all point the way. An especially good category to check out is favorite quotes.

Years ago when I was in college, I purchased a small, blank, fabric-covered book and began to record my favorite quotes from reading assignments, professors, posters, and friends' poetry. Recently, my daughter shared with me her own small, fabric-covered book filled with favorite quotes, not knowing about the one I had kept. We swapped books and quietly read each other's cherished personal wisdom.

Almost thirty years separate the two collections. Times have changed and so have many of the quote sources. (For instance, my book cites the music of Laura Nyro; my daughter includes lyrics by Dave Matthews.) But what surprised me pleasantly was the character of the content. Whether we both recorded Greek philosophers or modern-day songwriters, the messages were the same.

I believe that it's important to surround yourself with supportive reminders of what you hold to be true today. Unfortunately, it's very easy to feel clear and centered in the morning and then by noon be disoriented and in crisis-management mode. But if you can look up and see a Post-It note or framed message that reminds you to take a deep breath or even just to smile, it's a gentle push to get yourself back on track.

✎ Something I've Made

Another favorite group assignment is to "bring in something you've made." This can be anything you've constructed with your two hands—that you've baked, sewn, painted, photographed, written, or drawn. You can have made it this morning or thirty years ago.

45

Invariably, this exercise highlights hidden talents, because everyone is creative at something. Once again, you discover who you are, this time through the medium of your creativity.

✎ *My Drainers and Fillers*

This exercise has to do with those activities, people, and places that *drain* your energy and those that *fill* you with energy.

On the next page in your notebook, make two lists—one of your Drainers and the other of your Fillers. Be totally honest about which items go where on your lists; you won't be able to make improvements in how you spend your time unless you are. If you're uncertain about what to put where, keep a log for a day or two of the people with whom you spend any time (either in person or on the phone), and ask yourself how you feel after each interaction: drained, filled, or neutral. Your goal is to minimize interaction time with Drainers and know where to turn if you need some time with Fillers.

Knowing Your Needs

One reason it's important to know who you are currently is that not all advice is good for all people. This is especially true when it comes to organizing. Everyone has individual preferences and comfort levels, and that determination comes before deciding what systems and products will work for you.

Recently, a small headline in the morning paper caught my eye: "The Container Store Holds Grand Opening." For a professional organizer, this is an event that rates up there with a major movie premiere!

I drove over at the first opportunity, grabbed a shopping cart, and proceeded to stroll casually through the store. I wanted to appear professional, even though I was dying to run my hands over every Lucite, mesh, and wooden surface. There were clear containers and heavy metal ones, colorful cardboard and shiny white aluminum. There were boxes and bins and buckets of every size and shape.

It was an organizer's paradise, but judging from the confused expressions on many shoppers' faces, it was not a blissful experience for all. I was standing next to one young woman who had been staring at a display of multicolored hanging files and muttering to herself for quite some time. She would pick up a pack of one color, toss it into her cart, and then take it back out and replace it with another color. I introduced myself and asked if I could help. She said that she was a new police officer, and although they had taught her quite a bit at the police academy, they had neglected to include a class on filing, and she had no idea where to begin. Should "handcuffs" be filed alongside "drug busts"? Should "perpetrators" have their own section? What about "forensics"? Does she need to use different colors for every subject?

And that's the conundrum of shopping for organizational products. Specialty store chains ranging from Staples and Office Depot to Bed Bath & Beyond and Pottery Barn, plus all manner of getting-organized catalogues, feature potentially fabulous products in magnificent colors and styles. However, they provide virtually no clues as to how to use them or how to use them well, or even whether they *should* be used by someone with your particular needs.

For example, during my little trip I fell in love with several different models of CD and DVD storage systems. They were attractive and functional but were either too large to fit my space or required some sort of assembly that I didn't want to be bothered with. Had I not been very clear on what I needed, I could have been seduced easily by an expensive floor model.

There were so many items in the store that were fun to imagine having. I especially liked the clear, hinged plastic boxes with different-size compartments. They started off with full-drawer size and then worked downward (by divisions into halves, quarters, eighths), and then the container itself shrank until finally there was just one little marble-sized box. These clear boxes are especially good for organizing jewelry. Storage is efficient, with no wasted space or tangling, and everything is visible.

Visibility is an important consideration for those individuals who subscribe to the "out of sight, out of mind" theory. Although there are now any number of solid-colored containers in which to put items, Lucite and clear plastic are still the best bet for "everything out" types. "Nothing out" types have more leeway in their choices but are advised to label the contents of their storage systems so as not to be faced later with hidden miscellaneous hodgepodges.

Shopping in The Container Store can be a mystical or mystifying experience, depending on where you're coming from. The best-looking stuff may not be the best for you if it doesn't complement your environment and organizational personality. So heed the maxim, Know Thyself and Thy Needs, before investing in any new product or system.

Gifts Come in Strange Packages

A good friend had been experiencing a confusing mix of what would appear to be setbacks and problems and was wondering what she'd been doing wrong. "Maybe it's my karma," she sighed over the phone, giving an audible shrug.

"I don't think so," I reassured her. "Sounds more like lessons to me." She was not exactly thrilled with this response.

"You're probably right," she admitted reluctantly, "but it's just not fair. I've been trying so hard, and then I get socked with all this."

Does this sound familiar? "It's just not fair" is a universal lament, and we all know the correct comeback line: "Life *isn't* fair." So what can we do with that information? The answer is, "A lot."

Life's challenges give us the opportunity to see what we're made of and what we need to work on. There are, of course, some challenges that come in the form of terrible tragedies that boggle the mind, but for most of us, most of the time, our challenges are really gifts in disguise that teach us what we need to know to become stronger, kinder, and better people.

And our most common challenges are rarely total surprises. They're the same issues, coming up again and again in different forms, until we're ready to deal with them. For instance, have you ever left one job, or two or three, only to find yourself dealing with the same kinds of irritating people wherever you go? Or how many times have you thought you've successfully sidestepped an uncomfortable situation, only to discover that it somehow keeps reappearing?

Life's challenges are really gifts—the universe's way of nudging us in the right direction. Another friend of mine literally needed to be hit in the head before she could "get it." She had been procrastinating, for seemingly good reasons, on following up on a volunteer opportunity involving her dog, and as we were talking about it over the phone she suddenly yelled, "OW!" It turns out that her son had tossed a toy to the dog, missed, and accidentally bopped his mom on the head with it.

They say you can run but you can't hide, and there's probably a lot of truth to that. Sometimes we're not aware of when we're avoiding something, but often we do know, deep down, when we're not being honest with ourselves. Yes, confronting difficult situations can be tough, but the cost of denial can be equally tough.

Recognizing Gifts in Disguise

Here's where the concept of "gifts" comes in. If you can reframe your difficult experiences and instead of saying, "All I ever get is grief" (even if it truly feels that way) and instead ask, "OK, what, exactly, is going on here?" you then have the opportunity to discover whether, in fact, there is a lesson involved that you can master and move past. We get these gifts (or opportunities) every day but seldom take the time to step back and see if there's a pattern that we can discern and do something about.

We are not victims. Much of what happens to us has to do with our belief systems and how much responsibility we're prepared to take for our actions or nonactions. No, we can't control or prevent everything unpleasant, but we can ask ourselves whether we may be contributing to our own problems.

I had a client who was one of those individuals things kept happening to. He was always shaking his head in disbelief at the "total incompetence" of the people he was forced to deal with. He complained that he always wound up in the wrong lines at the bank and supermarket check-out, was always getting the seat on the plane next to the crying baby or the person who couldn't stop coughing. He was constantly running behind schedule because no one knew how to do his or her job efficiently. Wherever he went, automatic teller machines malfunctioned and faxes got jammed. And so forth and so on.

Now, was he experiencing an unbelievable run of bad luck or the power of expectation? I believe it was the latter—that he did (and we all do) exert a strong influence on what happened to him, simply through the nature of his beliefs. We end up seeing a lot of what we expect to see in life.

It's been said that by changing your thoughts you can change your world. For starters, I do know that when I change my interpretation of events, I can experience more peace. When I don't automatically assume that my kids are out to get me when they revise schedules at the last minute and try rolling with it all instead, I process my frustration in a healthier way. "Life is not a crisis," I tell myself, "nor is everything unplanned an emergency. This is just another opportunity for you to show that you understand that, Sunny."

Not every cloud has that proverbial silver lining, but life's gifts are what you make of them. Examine the packages and see what you can find.

Expanding Your Boundaries

Part of your lifelong journey of self-discovery is learning what your boundaries are and why they're there. Certain boundaries are good to have; they help you maintain your integrity and self-respect. But other self-imposed limits may be holding you back and need to be examined.

How you define yourself has a lot to do with where you've set your limits. To say, "I don't cook," "I'm not an artist," "I have no time to exercise," "I can't sing," "I'm too scared to swim," or "I'm a lousy typist" means that you have a perception of your capabilities based on messages you've given yourself and accepted as truth. But the fact is, there is a whole world of possibilities out there that you've chosen not to experience. And that's OK too, unless there's something that you very much want to do but are afraid to try.

That's why I'm proposing a "step challenge"—a series of one-by-one baby steps to get you moving toward an enticing goal that seems just out of your reach because of entrenched beliefs about your capabilities.

As an example, it's been a long road for me to accept the idea of myself as a writer. I've progressed far enough to be comfortable with the idea of being a "nonfiction writer," but that's as far as it's gone. Now, however, I'm looking at the label of "potential fiction writer."

A writer's message board that I post to has suggested that the group do a round-robin story between partners, with one person writing a paragraph and then shipping it off to the other person to add a paragraph and then send it back. I wasn't sure that I could or should participate, being a non-fiction writer, but one wonderful member bypassed that concern by e-mailing me the first paragraph of "our" story, which launched the old $64,000 question: "Who am I to think I can write fiction?"

And this is where I initiated my own step challenge. If I think that I might be interested in fiction writing, a marvelous yet safe place to get my feet wet would be among friends in this writer's group. Starting with simple back-and-forth paragraphs and learning from what my partner writes, I can give it a whirl and see how I feel.

I presented this idea at one of my Organizing for the Spirit groups and received a lot of encouragement. And we all decided to commit ourselves, before the next meeting, to taking one step in a direction in which we would like to go but that may be causing us some anxiety.

One group member who was working on spring cleaning has a large house but admitted being uncomfortable tackling a back staircase that was jammed with stuff from her last job. Her first step was to invite me over to see if I had any suggestions about long-term storage for archived material. Another member was stuck in the initial stages of a difficult memoir she desperately wanted to write and found herself allowing distractions to interfere with her writing time. Her first step was to commit to writing a certain number of pages by our next meeting. A third member was having difficulty carving out time to plan for a possible entrepreneurial business, because her demanding full-time workdays left her with too little energy. Her first step was to block out time from her weekends.

First steps can be liberating if they're small and doable, and that's the intention. I don't have to decide today—or ever—that I'm going to be a fiction writer, only that I'm going to do a little fiction writing with a friend. In the process, I can see whether I like it and whether I'd like to take further steps on this path.

To explore the possibilities is the goal, and to get there you sometimes have to move past old, outmoded boundaries. Let your spirit direct you where to go and what personal limits to challenge. Remember, it's never too late to start becoming who you really are.

✎ One Step Toward My Goal

Decide on something that is calling to you—a cherished dream, a whisper of possibility, an exciting offer—and see how you can move one step in that direction. The only criterion is that the activity should be something that appeals to you rather than an obligation.

From this chapter, I hope you have a better idea of *who* you are. The next step is to focus your attention on being *where* you are.

4

Be Where You Are

Aman named Charles Flandrau expressed this concept well when he said, years ago: "Life does not consist either in wallowing in the past or of peering anxiously at the future. It is good for one to appreciate that life is now. Whatever it offers, little or much, life is now this day—this hour. As the doctor said to the woman who complained that she did not like the night air: 'Madam, during certain hours of the twenty-four, night air is the only air there is.'"

The more we can value and appreciate where we are at the moment, the greater our happiness. And the more we can practice patience, trust, and the simple act of breathing, the easier it will be to get things done.

PAY ATTENTION THROUGH WRITING A COLUMN

Writing a column is a good exercise for sensitizing you to the present moment and enabling you to look at things with a fresh eye. It doesn't matter if you think you can't write. The purpose is to find something—anything—that piques your interest and then explore your thoughts and feelings on the subject.

Writing a column forces you to examine your life with patient curiosity. Normally, we're doing anything but that. We bounce off of our environment like shots in a pinball game, hurtling from one bumper to another.

When you slow down and deliberately take notice of your surroundings, you're in the present moment, and being in the present moment brings things into sharper focus. It's as though you're on a nature expedition, but you're using your binoculars to observe the details of your *own* life.

How often do we actually question why we do things the way we do? One way to get inside ourselves is to pretend that we're entertaining visitors from another planet who want to better understand our way of life. Imagine that they're looking for simple explanations of our daily routines, such as the reasoning behind our nighttime beauty rituals or who takes out the garbage and why.

It can be amazing to discover how much we do automatically, out of habit. I first became aware of this phenomenon years ago, when I was living in a small apartment. Each week, I would put out a fresh set of towels in the bathroom. The closet shelf that the towels were on was very narrow so that every time I pulled out a few, the other towels would fall onto the floor. I would pick them up, refold them, stack them back on the shelf, and close the door. One day, I took a closer look at the closet and saw that the other shelves were wider than the one the towels were on. Instead of just mindlessly picking up the dropped towels, refolding and re-storing them, I could make my life easier by putting them on one of the wider shelves where they wouldn't be jumping out all the time.

Taking the time to examine an old routine can be very practical. But it's also beneficial to make the time to look at everything more closely—your bookshelves, your best friend, your yellow Labrador, your front steps. And how about listening? When did you last pay attention to the sounds in your yard at night? The background vocals on an old-favorite CD? The laughter of schoolchildren playing outside after lunch? The sound of leaves crunching on the pavement? And what about the smells and tastes of a summer-fresh peach or just-baked pumpkin pie?

This is what you do when you write a column. You pay attention. You observe. You figure out what you think and how you feel about what you're observing. Another benefit of writing a column is that, by definition, you're limited to a certain number of words. So not only are you collecting your thoughts, you're prioritizing them. The act of counting words keeps you close to your center; you have to keep peeling away layers to get to the kernel of truth before you run out of room.

Much of our day-to-day business can be done by rote. But when we're fully engaged, active participants in moment-by-moment creation, we're in the state linked most closely to "living" our lives. To be a human being means to be totally present as much as you can. This means to be where you are, no matter where that is. When you're eating, you're eating. When you're listening to your child, you're listening to your child. When you're playing the guitar, you're not doing anything else with your fingers, eyes, or emotions.

✎ *My Favorite Time*

Block out about forty-five minutes when you won't be interrupted. In your notebook, write a column on the subject of your favorite time of day. Aim for between five hundred to eight hundred words in which you describe the sights, sounds, and feel of that time period and what makes it so special for you.

ORGANIZING FOR THE SEASON

How often do we let the seasons whiz by without actually being present for them? So many times we wake up at the end of summer, fall, winter, or spring and say to ourselves, "Darn! I wanted to do so much and now it's too late. Guess I'll just have to wait until next year."

Here's a way to stop that cycle.

✎ *My Favorite Season*

Let's say fall is arriving soon. I want you to think of one thing—just one—that you enjoy about this season. Perhaps you welcome the sudden crispness of the air, the cooler nights, and warm, comforting clothes. Maybe you look forward to Halloween and caramel apples or candy corn. Or you could just enjoy the relief of the kids being back in school so you have more time to yourself.

Once you've identified your "something," I'd like you to open your notebook and write down how you can enjoy fall to the utmost. Can you bring more of it into your life? Can you plan a special ritual to make it stand out? Can you use your time in such a way that when fall turns into winter, you'll be able to say, "I was present for the season this year. I didn't let it get away from me."

You could plan a road trip to watch the leaves change, take photos, or do sketches. You could make hot apple cider with cinnamon sticks or a pot of homemade soup; you could shop for a down comforter; you could throw a party. There are so many ideas to choose from, especially in seasonal magazines. The "what" you do doesn't matter as much as your attitude and effort.

I know it isn't easy to focus on the moment, although we may understand that it's the only sane and sensible way to enjoy our lives. But what we can do is, at least, to live in the season we're in and take some joy in the progression of nature. We can let our senses be stimulated by what's happening in our own neighborhoods and backyards. We can think about what makes fall what it is and *be there* for it.

Of course, this will take some organization, because the primary reason we don't do these things already is that we go around muttering to ourselves, "It's not my fault. I simply don't have enough time." And you know what the answer to that is. No one has "enough" time, but everyone has all the time there is. It boils down to understanding what's significant in your life and planning what you do accordingly.

Make a list of your favorite activities associated with fall and put it side-by-side with your weekly to-do list. Assuming that you accept the concept that your own needs are as vital as anyone else's, what can you manage to put aside or do differently so that you can create time for a seasonal

Organizing for the Spirit

pleasure? What can be eliminated, delegated, done more efficiently, or done at another time?

Once you've learned how to plan for seasonal enjoyment, it's not too difficult to think in terms of a given day, a
week, or even a month. It's important to give yourself meaningful activities to look forward to. It's not sufficient to read
an article or a book and say, "I want to do more of the things
that are important to me" and then just turn the page.

✎ *Pleasures of the Season*
Start a section in your notebook for "Pleasures of the Season."
Title a page for each of the four seasons, and whenever you
remember something pleasurable associated with that particular
season, add it to the list.

PRACTICING PATIENCE

The more you can accept and appreciate the current circumstances of your life, the better position you will be in to effect
change in the future. In other words, don't fight reality; deal
with it. There truly is a season for everything, if you can hang
in there long enough.

Occasionally, when progress toward a goal is super slow,
we find that we're going about things the wrong way and we
have to make some adjustments to keep on track. But more
often than not, we're actually butting our heads against the
wrong doors or expecting those doors to open more quickly. We're too attached to the outcomes we've pictured in our
heads to allow events to unfold any differently, and in this
way we create our own problems.

For example, I had a client who was determined to redecorate her apartment. But every time she started to seriously shop for new furniture, she ran into obstacles: she experienced a time crunch at work; she came down with the flu; she received some unexpected bills. And then one day, she was offered a business promotion if she would be willing to move to another city. She jumped at the prospect and used her savings to purchase an ideally located townhouse—an opportunity she wouldn't have been able to take advantage of, financially, had she pushed on with her redecorating plan.

Was it just a happy coincidence? I don't think so. When we can step back and look at our situations more objectively, we can often see that we're being encouraged toward, or discouraged from, a particular path, and we have the opportunity to adjust accordingly.

Detachment is the art of separating ourselves from our "needs" long enough to evaluate the appropriateness of our actions. What messages are we getting that tell us whether we're heading in the right direction or not? Are we listening to those messages? Are we heeding them? Although it's essential to develop the skills of good goal setting and planning, it's just as important to have the flexibility and patience to know when to readjust those plans, based on the feedback we're receiving.

Most of us tend to get a little stubborn at times. We want what we want when we want it, especially when we've been working very hard or without a break. These are the times that test our patience the most and yet, paradoxically, can bring us the greatest rewards if we can manage to flow with the current just a little longer. An outcome even better than we had imagined could be just around the corner. Or possibly, the avoidance of a disaster could await. You probably can recall stories of people who missed airplane connections and whose lives were spared when the plane they were supposed to be on went down.

The bottom line is that we don't always know why events are transpiring the way they are. If we can exercise patience, instead of forcing the issue, and pay attention to the messages of the moment, we have a better chance of finding out the reasons and receiving assistance along the way.

SHIFTING PERSPECTIVE

I don't like to go food shopping. As hard as I try not to, I find myself getting impatient with crowded aisles, slow-moving carts, and malfunctioning scanners. I was sharing my resignation at having to go to the grocery store yet again with a family friend (who is in his late seventies), when he said quietly to me, "You have no idea how lucky you really are." I looked at him with surprise, and he went on to tell me about what he experienced when he came to the United States from Europe after World War II and went food shopping here for the first time. He described his amazement at seeing the fully stocked markets and how wonderful it was to be able to make selections from so many different possibilities. "You know," he finished with a smile, "you truly are fortunate to have this kind of a problem." Well, there wasn't much for me to say after that. But he certainly gave me some food for thought.

This conversation took place a while ago, and I wish I could say that I've learned to appreciate my large biweekly shopping trips more. I'm still reluctant to go, but looking at it through my friend's eyes was definitely enlightening. It's just so easy to be cemented to whatever old perspective you're used to.

And this applies to everything from perspectives on shopping, to perspectives on the state of the union, child-rearing approaches, and even weather predictions. In Baltimore, Maryland, my hometown, it's known and understood that the natives will panic at the mere mention of snow in the forecast. Shelves have to be stocked with provisions (especially toilet paper), and gas tanks must be topped off. Everything goes into a heightened state of readiness when *it's going to snow*. Never mind that Baltimoreans have survived numerous blizzards. It's the notification of the first inch that causes the panic, because people don't seem to remember that they do know how to get around in the snow. Old fears and faulty perceptions limit their perspective.

The only way to get a new perspective is to take a step in a different direction. Moving in any direction will allow you to view the same situation from an alternate angle, and the tiniest shift can be significant.

This understanding came to me in a very literal way when I was visiting Roanji Temple in Kyoto, Japan, a number of years ago. There's a famous Zen garden in Kyoto, which contains nothing but white sand and fifteen rocks. The garden is walled in on two sides but can be viewed from different vantage points on the other two sides. What's fascinating is that no matter where you sit to look at the garden, there's no place where you can see all fifteen rocks at the same time. At least one rock is always hidden behind another.

We were told that this garden is a representation of the belief that not everything in life is visible, that is, not everything can be known to us. Depending on where you're situated, you will always be presented with a view that is somewhat limited, and only by shifting your perspective can you see what you were not able to see before.

Have you thought about where your own perspective might benefit from a little shifting? One exercise that can be very useful is to take another person's side in a discussion and argue the issue from that point of view. Granted, it may not be fun to have to put forth arguments that you may strongly disagree with, but debaters do it all the time. This technique encourages flexible and open thinking and gives you insights that you might not be receptive to in any other format.

Another option is to move yourself physically to another position. When my son got his learner's permit, I realized that I was no longer in the driver's seat (so to speak). Riding in the car as a passenger and watching him navigate traffic showed me the reality of what it means to let go and let him make his own path through life. What's interesting is that I had to move to the other seat—literally, physically—to see that so clearly.

Whether the shift is physical or emotional, there's still movement. And once you've experienced something differently, even for just a moment, you will never be entirely the same. That new awareness opens you up to other ways of thinking, as well as to options for growth and change. It can occur in an instant and last a lifetime.

LIVING IN PROCRASTINATIONLAND

Putting things off and wandering around under the cloud of anxiety caused by putting them off can greatly affect our ability to enjoy the present moment. For instance, there are generally two types of people when it comes to tax season: those who deal with April 15th in January and those who deal with April 15th on April 14th. Yes, some of us fall in the middle, but if, by the end of March, you're just getting around to beginning to think about the possibility of doing your taxes, you qualify for membership in the second group.

The thought of dealing with taxes is usually not a pleasant one, especially if you do not expect to receive a refund. And what do we tend to do with unpleasant thoughts? We shove them into a tiny mental closet and try not to have anything to do with them until or unless they ooze out from under that closet door.

The mind games that we play to avoid doing what we don't feel like doing can be truly amazing. They can even surpass the complexity of the task itself. To give you an example: I'm five feet tall. Most pairs of slacks that I buy need to be shortened, which means making occasional trips to the seamstress. This is not very difficult to do, in and of itself, but I tend to put it off.

This brings us to the secondary difficulty in procrastinating: the act of putting something off engenders its own guilt and makes us uncomfortable. We then try not to think about the fact that we're not doing what we're supposed to be doing. So my bag of unaltered clothes has now morphed into a guilt trip, which totally bypasses the logic that I'm putting off something that I need to do and want to do, and the doing of which will make me very happy.

At this juncture in ProcrastinationLand, it should be obvious that it would be easier to just go ahead and do what I'm putting off rather than to continue to avoid it. Oh, but no! By this time, I've had a go at the "Drink Me" bottle that makes things appear much larger than they normally are. The simple little prospect of dashing in and out of the seamstress's place has become overwhelming. I think about it every time I walk by the bag of clothes, and every time I drive by her storefront, and when I see her somewhere else in town. ("Off with her head!") This undone task is haunting me, and I want out.

And then one day I have nothing to wear, or so it seems. I go to the seamstress with my bag of clothes and have them altered. The End.

Why do I do this to myself? Why do any of us put off things that have to be done eventually, aggravating ourselves unnecessarily in the process, especially when they're not that big a deal to being with? (In my case, I believe it has to do with my seamstress's location in the dry cleaner's shop and how uncomfortable the very small dressing room is there.)

There can be a number of psychological reasons why people procrastinate in general, but when it comes to taxes, one of the main reasons is disorganization. When systems aren't set up and active during the year, the thought of tackling the paperwork preparation can be overwhelming. It can be "taxing" enough to have to go to your accountant to see what you may owe, but the anticipation becomes much worse when you don't know whether you can find what you need to substantiate legitimate claims.

My hat goes off to the legion of dedicated accountants who calmly and patiently hold their clients' hands and explain for the umpteenth time that the process would go much more smoothly if the clients would only keep records *throughout* the year. Even a simple $10 accordion file, divided by tax categories, would make everyone's life easier.

So why is it so hard for some people to follow that suggestion? It's hard for the same reason I didn't get my bag of clothes out of the house. In ProcrastinationLand, nothing is what it seems. Many things appear to be much larger, but some actually appear to be smaller than they are—so small, in fact, that we're sure we can dispatch them quickly at a later date. We put them off, and when the time comes to deal with them, we find that we've left out a good part of the equation. And, unfortunately, there aren't enough hours left to do the job right.

When we're lost in ProcrastinationLand, having good organizational systems to fall back on is key. We all put things off from time to time, but the fact is that being able to find what we need to find, in the time available to find it, allows us to do what we need to do in the time available to do it.

There's no time like the present!

✎ *Things I've Been Putting Off*
In your notebook, make a list of everything you've been putting
off. Analyze each one, honestly, to determine the reason you've
been putting it off. Is it that it's too large and you don't know
where to start? Do you not have the necessary materials? Is there
too much work involved for one person? Do you dislike the job
or the people involved? Are you having trouble coming up with a
time to do it? Are you waiting to be in the right mood? Does it
still need to be done? Does it need to be done by *you*?

Depending on your answer for each item, devise a strategy to
move you forward on the accomplishment of that task.

BREATHING IN THE PRESENT MOMENT

Few things bring you back to where you are as quickly as a
health problem. As we all know but seldom remember, we
tend to take our health for granted until we lose it for any
length of time.

I was battling bronchitis in the dead of winter, and
although it wasn't life-threatening, it certainly grabbed my
attention and made me appreciate the little things in life—
like swallowing without pain, being able to hear out of both
ears, going whole days without crippling sinus headaches or
coughing, and, most of all, unimpeded breathing.

Having to focus on your breath definitely takes you back
to the essentials. The first day I got out of bed and came
down to my office, I gingerly sat down at my desk, trying not
to cough. I'd found that moving slowly enabled me to do little things without aggravating my cough center.

However, I was not expecting the other benefits that came along with my measured breathing. As I was sitting there, updating addresses and phone numbers in my various books, I happened to look up and see snow gently falling on the trees extending over my patio. It was so interesting. It looked as though it was happening in slow motion. The snowflakes seemed unusually soft and delicate, and the evergreen never looked so green. I was mesmerized.

It took me a while to realize that my perceptions were being altered by my slow movements and careful breathing. I was totally in the present moment, not pushing myself but genuinely, absolutely there.

I've always embraced the importance of being in the Now, but there's a difference between doing it at a high energy level rather than a low one. Instead of just pausing to appreciate the moment, I *was* the moment because I couldn't be doing anything else.

It was an "Ah-ha!" of significant proportions. Could this be the universe's way of telling me something? Normally I, like most people I know, operate at a fair rate of speed. If I'm not doing something, then I'm thinking about what I have to do. I've learned to stop and enjoy the little commas of beauty and humor and kindness during my day, but I'm still moving at a good clip when I do. What if I simply slowed down to the pace of my breathing and experienced things from that vantage point?

My first thought was, "How in the world can I go slower? There's too much to accomplish!" But then, I thought about my mental state after I had finished observing the snow on the patio. I was calm, relaxed—and crystal clear. Sharp. I moved through the afternoon like that, pacing myself but enjoying what I did. I knew that I was not capable of overextending myself in any way, and my body cooperated by letting me know when it was time to stop.

Believe it or not, that was one of the most productive afternoons I have ever had. I was totally involved with what I had before me, because I didn't have the energy to be anywhere else.

Lesson? I probably don't have to get sick to experience that. The reason I think this "slowed to the rhythm of breathing" approach might work is that I can see the results. No, you may not get as much done as you would if you raced around like a demented hamster, but two things would definitely happen instead. One, you wouldn't be so exhausted at the end of the day, and two, the pay-off for your efforts would justify the slow-down. You'd have more quality work to show for your time and would be taking better care of yourself to boot.

What does it take to remember this? We're challenged at every turn to entrain ourselves to the beat of our times. We're encouraged to do more and move faster. It's hard to swim against this tide, but if we realize that slowing down actually can work to our advantage, we may be encouraged to give it a try. Seeing snow fall, flake by flake, is a magical experience. And so is doing what we need to do in a way that enhances our sense of well-being.

It's easy to give it a whirl. Just stop and breathe.

KNOWING THE IMPORTANCE OF TRUST

Being where we are means that we face up to whatever is transpiring in the present moment, as unpleasant as that may be.

Several years ago, a series of unexpected events tossed me out of "life cruise" mode and into the cold rapids of uncharted reality. A good friend counseled me to grab onto the only thing I could—my faith that things would work out the way they were supposed to—and just hang on. In other words, use trust as my life preserver.

Crises test our beliefs, and I believe that they occur when they do as a way of showing us what we're made of; they make us walk our talk and demonstrate how far we've come since the last time our foundation was shaken. We'd much rather do without them, of course, but handled correctly, they can lift us to the next level of our growth.

Crises can range from small, unpleasant surprises to (literally) earth-shattering events. We may just be knocked off balance or thrown to the ground. But in every case, our feelings of security are at least momentarily derailed. And that's what can prove so terrifying.

"This isn't supposed to be happening," we tell ourselves. "I didn't bargain for this; I didn't plan for it. I did everything I was supposed to do and knew how to do. It isn't fair." We've all experienced the shock and disbelief of events occurring, big or little, for which we don't feel prepared. Our first reaction usually is to fight the unwelcome reality, but our success in dealing with it will, in large part, depend on how quickly we can move to the next stage: acknowledgment.

With acknowledgment comes the acceptance that yes, the event has indeed occurred. We are no longer on the boat; we are in the rapids. And we have a choice: we can resist by frantically attempting to swim upstream or we can flow with the current and see what our options are. And to flow or float, we need a life preserver.

By accepting trust as that life preserver, we're enabling ourselves to relax and assess the situation without wasting all of our energy flailing about. We need that energy and all of our wits about us, because sometimes we're tossed overboard for a reason that's not immediately apparent. Very often, there's something hidden in the depths that can be of use to us, but when we refuse to accept that a change or reversal has happened, we limit our ability to learn or develop or benefit from the knowledge we gain. If you can trust that things do often happen for a reason, you're in a position to observe from a different perspective and look for whatever messages there might be for you.

Sometimes the message is that we should be doing things differently. Maybe we need to appreciate certain things more. Or certain people. Maybe we're being told that our timing isn't right. Maybe we have to learn the value of patience, or honesty, or kindness, or self-love, or humor. Maybe we just have to learn to weather adversity with dignity and faith.

Having trust doesn't mean that everything will necessarily work out the way you want it to. Having trust means that you accept the reality of where you are at the present moment yet know that you are being supported through your ordeal and that if you are patient and perceptive, you'll find a way to persevere. You'll come out stronger, maybe wiser, and hopefully with a greater sense of peace.

✎ *An Experience of Trusting*
   In your notebook, recall a time when you had to surrender con-
   trol and trust that things would work out for the highest good.
   Write about that experience and what you learned from it.

BECOMING AWARE OF SYNCHRONICITIES

Personal growth often operates in cycles. There are times when we are very other-oriented, that is, focusing on external variables, and other times when we're more willing or able to turn inward. One way of noting if you are on an inward track is to check out your awareness of synchronicities.

Synchronicities are meaningful coincidences whose implications can be astounding. For example, I'm sure that you have, at one time or the other, thought of someone you haven't heard from in quite a while, only to have that person miraculously contact you a short time later. What makes this event worth paying close attention to is its potential "meaning." Maybe your caller happens to hold a key to a significant event currently unfolding in your life; maybe she or he has important information for you, or perhaps will even point you in a direction that you should be headed.

Not too long ago, as I was gathering my materials for a workshop I was about to conduct, I felt a "nudge" to bring along a certain book that I had not been planning to take. I stuffed it into my briefcase and didn't think any more about it until the group was in the middle of a discussion. Suddenly, I could see a connection between what one of the attendees was saying and the subject of the book. I pulled it out, showed it to her, and she looked at me in shock. She couldn't believe that I was holding a book that had been so transformative in her life at one time but whose inspirational teachings she had long since forgotten about. She knew, immediately and intuitively, that this was a sign to remind her of what is important to her and that she should stay conscious of this.

And I knew that it was a sign for me, too. Whenever I pay attention to "connections," not just my own but others' as well, I see patterns that can be rich in meaning. I believe that these connective patterns exist whether we pay attention to them or not, so we might as well make use of the additional information.

You may ask, "How do I know if what happens to me is a true synchronicity or only a coincidence?" And again, the answer lies in your own sense of meaning. It may feel like the universe is just giving you a humorous little wink, or you may feel something deeper, something more profound and moving. You may experience wonder and even excitement. These are signals to look more closely and see what's in your spiritual mailbox today.

If at this particular time you are experiencing the flip side of these feelings, that's still information for you. If your positive synchronicity sightings are far apart, it might be a message that you're not on track with what you ought to be doing. You need to pay attention to whatever is unfolding in your life, whether those events are planned or unplanned. Some of your most valuable revelations can come from what you didn't want to happen or what you didn't expect. There are messages everywhere, if you slow down and take a good look.

Make time to center yourself each day. Make sure you're peaceful and open enough to be able to recognize a sign when you see one. You can't force a response, but you can create the conditions in which it will be easier to perceive messages. For some of us, that may mean clearing our minds while running, steaming out tension in the shower, or even taking deep breaths while stuck in traffic and then noticing what bumper stickers or billboards are around you. Signs can take many different forms.

Experiencing synchronicities is only possible if you're conscious of where you are.

✎ *A Synchronicities Record*

Turn to a fresh page in your notebook, and start to keep track of these synchronicities when you become aware of them. Try to correlate them with what is going on in your life at the time. Connections may be immediate, or it may take much longer to understand how you're being guided, but trust the process. It's a major highway to happiness.

REMOVING THE DEADWOOD

It can be hard to appreciate where we are if we can't see the forest for the trees . . . A few years ago, my group of trees were suddenly gone, every one. The tall, beautiful hemlocks that edged my patio had been dying for several years—victims of an incurable disease that transformed their hardy green branches into empty brown twigs.

I resisted, but we finally had to have them cut down, and all of a sudden I could see into my neighbors' yards and into their houses, and this was very interesting. No, not because I am a nosey busybody but because, although I've always been one to treasure my privacy, at the same time I'm incredibly curious about the rest of the world. So while we waited for the new bushes to be planted and grow, instead of staring out at a wall of green, I found myself enjoying the antics of children on their sliding board and watching retirees relax in the springtime sun, reading the newspaper.

Sitting at my desk and taking in this scene one day, I began to think about why I'm so fascinated with what people do and how they do it. It truly is the foundation of my organizing and coaching business, and it's why I see everything as connected: how people spend their time, what sorts of dishes and pens they like to use, what papers they save, what magazines they look at, the things they collect, the music they listen to, the stuff on their closet floor—all are evidence of unique personalities.

Although it's fine to improve your organizational skills purely for productivity's sake—to be more efficient, effective, streamlined, and functional—the bottom line is how everything fits together in the jigsaw puzzle that's your life. The goal should not be just to have the pieces fit well but to produce a picture that's pleasing and that's truly you—you today.

And that's why we need to clean out the deadwood once in a while—so we can get a clear view of what's actually there now. Removing the deadwood is not always the easiest thing to do, especially for pack rats. We get very used to having our belongings around, even if they're serving no useful purpose. That was the case with my hemlocks. When I thought of the years I'd spent staring out at them while I worked and all of the experiences I've had that they'd borne silent witness to, the idea of chopping them down seemed impossible. But that was then, and this is now.

And that is one of the keys to being able to part with things. Often it's not the things themselves but the memories they represent that we're holding onto. But memories can be preserved in other ways, such as in pictures. So many times when I've run out of space to store items and have to make choices about what to save and what to get rid of, I've taken a picture—of my favorite raggedy Mickey Mouse sweatshirt, a shelf of old college texts, a broken baby toy. And my row of hemlocks.

Through the years, I'd taken many pictures of them through the patio doors—pictures of them loaded with snow and sheltering a cardinal or two, and several showing the soft shadows they cast in the summer sun. And those are what I remembered as their remains were taken down. And now, there were bright open spaces, waiting for new bushes to grow and a whole new view of the landscape. That's the upside of getting rid of your deadwood—cleared spaces to keep clear or fill with whatever gives you pleasure today.

Organizing is definitely a means toward an end, and not just an end in itself. As teachers of Feng Shui know, everything has its own energy, and working with that energy in a positive way can make a significant difference in your life.

Keeping things around you that are broken and unfixable, dirty or disorganized is not a good way to keep your energy flowing and healthy.

Think of organizing as a way of removing the deadwood that blocks your perception of your best self, and enjoy the present-day vistas that emerge!

ASKING THE RIGHT QUESTIONS

We were midway through the summer, and it was time for that annual August ritual in my house: And Where Are We Now? Actually, it's called Getting Your Room Cleaned Out Before School Starts, but I prefer to think of it as a seasonal rite of passage that enables me, for a brief moment, to peer into the hidden recesses of my children's developing personalities.

The purpose of the activity is two-fold: not only to create space in their closets and drawers and shelves for the accumulations of the next school year but to show them how to evaluate whether the things they own still have meaning to them. To me, this is the bedrock of organizational decision making and the most critical skill I can teach in this area.

When they were younger, we used to spend maybe an hour each day, for one week in August, going through toy boxes and bookcases and under-the-bed containers. We'd try to remember when they got their coloring books and who gave them that stuffed rabbit and how much fun they had collecting their Trolls. As they grew older, we sorted through Barbies and Teen-Age Mutant Ninja Turtles, stickers and dinosaurs, then later their Goosebump books and POGS and charm bracelets and plastic bugs. I will always treasure those moments, sitting on the floor in their rooms, listening to them reminisce about their favorite toys, their family, and their friends.

As we reviewed each item, they would place it in one of four piles:

1. To throw out because the item has outlived its usefulness or interest and isn't in good enough condition to pass along to someone else
2. To give to a friend or donate to a charity
3. To pack up for storage memories
4. To keep in their room because they enjoy using the item or looking at it

This was a very basic system that they had no trouble adapting to suit their personal needs, and as time passed, they said they found it easy enough to do on their own. In analyzing this approach, I think the reason it's so effective is that it asks the right questions.

Figuring out what to do with something—to discard, donate, put away, display—is usually not that difficult once you realize that you have the answers inside of yourself and you just need to be able to access that information. As has been said, it's a fact of life that nothing stays exactly the same. And that's certainly true of the value of the things you bring into your home. What once was a fun, fresh reminder of a special day or person might have become less important or simply worn out. With space in most places today at a premium, it makes sense to stay current with what you keep around you and move less treasured items out of prime real estate locations.

If everything seems equally valuable to you, you may want to try a ranking system to help discriminate. The items with the highest values stay within view or easy reach, and those with lower values get stored in less accessible places. Again, what's important here is your "dialogue" with yourself; the act of questioning and evaluating, based on *today's* needs and interests and priorities.

As we acquire and accumulate "stuff," it can feel overwhelming to look at it all, especially if we feel guilty about not using it or caring for it the way we could have. At times like these, it's important to remember to chop up big organizing jobs into manageable sizes and not to deal with guilt at all, if possible. Guilt just tires you out and doesn't help you make good decisions. If you find that guilt is slowing you down, I suggest that you imagine that you've just inherited your house from people you don't know and that whatever you discover there—undone, incomplete, sloppy, dirty, whatever—was not done by you and therefore is not your fault. Your only job is to make decisions about what you find, based on your lifestyle and preferences today. Ask yourself what works for you, what doesn't, and move on from there.

Learning how to talk to yourself productively, that is, to figure out how you *really* feel and what you *really* think, is critical in making effective choices in every area of your life. And asking yourself where you are at this point in time, in terms of what you're surrounding yourself with, is a great place to start.

As for me, although I sometimes miss those shared hours of reorganizing with my kids, it's good to see that they've gained the competence they need to tackle this lifelong job on their own. And as I watch them carefully place a cherished memento in a box headed for the attic or thoughtfully rearrange a desk display of photos of friends, my greatest pleasure comes from knowing that, for a moment at least, they're reflecting on what's truly important in life.

DOING YOUR NIGGLIES

At the opposite end from meaningful, enriching activities are the Nigglies of life. Nigglies are the endless small, bothersome tasks that take up residence on your to-do list but that you never seem to get around to doing, in part because they're so little. But being little doesn't keep them from being annoying, so after tripping over that pile in the corner of your entranceway for the tenth time this month, the hour has arrived to do something about it.

The nice thing about Nigglies is that it's easy to devote a solid chunk of time to getting rid of them. Example: In my kitchen, I've had a broken refrigerator magnet sitting on my countertop for ages, waiting for "someone" to glue it back together. Now that I'm ready to take care of it, the magnet part has somehow disappeared, leaving just the plastic surfboard. Now the decision to take care of it is easy: into the trash it goes. I'll just get another the next time I go to the beach. Easy, huh?

I've also had a decorative piece for my key chain sitting around waiting to be reattached. It's been waiting because fixing it meant that I had to find the needle-nosed pliers, which is a Niggly all by itself. Well, in doing my basement Nigglies, I located the pliers, and since it was Nigglies Day, I took it upstairs and fixed the key chain!

The trick here is a simple one: assigning a specific time to do Nigglies means that you're giving yourself permission to do small tasks that ordinarily you'd consider a waste of your prime time. By gearing yourself up to do as many as possible, you're making great use of your energy and eliminating aggravations in the process.

The whole family can get in on the act, and it's actually more fun to do Nigglies as a group. I asked my son what Nigglies he had waiting and, of course, they're the things on *my* list for him to do: putting the videos back in their boxes and hauling his clean laundry upstairs. (For some reason he doesn't mind getting dressed out of the dryer, but it bothers the heck out of me.)

The only time that doing Nigglies actually appeals to me is when I'm working on a large project, like writing a proposal. I'll sit down at the computer, look at the screen, and suddenly remember that the stapler needs more staples. And wasn't I going to change the sheets today? And how about running to the drug store for the odds and ends we need?

This is not the best approach. Sensible time management dictates some degree of discipline, and the fact of the matter is that Nigglies are best done in dedicated time periods. You can work off a list or write the tasks down on separate slips of paper and pick them from a jar. As mentioned, you can do them as a family group and follow up the Nigglies Day with some popcorn and a movie.

The major reason for devoting specific time to eliminating Nigglies is that they are greater than the sum of their parts. The smallest Nigglies can cause the biggest annoyances. I once waited to see how long it would take for someone else in my house to replace the roll of toilet paper when it was empty. Wouldn't you know it? Somehow a new roll appeared on the bathroom vanity and was used from there. For a day and a half. Yes, it does take five whole seconds to put a new roll on the roller, but apparently that was too much effort for some people.

There are very few better feelings, though, than getting rid of a recurring Niggly. What happens is that we forget about the Niggly until we stumble across it, then we rebuke ourselves for not taking care of it, and then we immediately put it out of our minds until the next time we trip over it. And so forth and so on. When we finally tackle the darn thing, the pleasure we receive from completing the action is way out of proportion to the action itself. Which makes us wonder, Why didn't we finish this six months ago?

The reason is that we're human. The most sensible goal would be to set regular time periods to do our Nigglies and not chastise ourselves in between. After all, we really don't want to end up with this commentary on our tombstones: "Got it all done. Died anyway."

Now it's time to kick back and look at the next cornerstone: enjoying your life.

5

Enjoy Your Life

Being able to enjoy your life means knowing what you need and believing that you can and must take good care of yourself. By making this a priority, you announce to yourself and the world that you value the quality time you schedule for yourself and understand that self-care is a gift to your spirit. Whether you yearn for more excitement or more serenity, the experience you desire is only a choice away.

LAUGHING AT ABSURDITY

It's important to have a good sense of humor. When was the last time you laughed really hard? When was the last time you laughed really hard at *yourself?*

If you're like the majority of us, you take yourself rather seriously most of the time. Life can be tough, for sure, and we do have to focus on making our way through difficult situations. But are all the situations we find ourselves in so very serious?

What would you do, for example, if you found out that you had accidentally shoplifted a tomato? That was the very circumstance my mother found herself in not too long ago. She was cruising the fruit and vegetable aisles in the supermarket and stopped to examine the tomatoes. My mother is not very tall, and she had to lean all the way forward to get to the best ones. Apparently, as she reached to the back of the bin, one of the tomatoes rolled down and dropped into the pocket of her jacket. She had no idea that this had happened until she paid for her groceries and went out to the car; when she put her hand into her pocket, she pulled out a tomato instead of her keys.

She stood there, she said, overcome with shock. My mother, who would never *ever* think of taking anything that was not rightfully hers, had just stolen a tomato.

She got this far in telling me the story, and I was already on the floor laughing so hard I couldn't breathe. These kinds of things happen to her all the time, and each new scenario is funnier than the last. Fortunately, my mother has a great sense of humor about herself and manages to survive these episodes with her ego intact.

Being able to laugh at yourself is a fundamental step on the road to enjoying your life. Either you learn to laugh at absurdity or you go down the drain with it. Perhaps if we all realized how often we do mindless things—spray our hair with bug spray, brush our teeth with BENGAY muscle ointment, gargle with wart medicine—we could take the whole human experience a little more lightly.

✎ *My Most Embarrassing Moments*
In your notebook, make a list of your most embarrassing moments and have a good laugh.

LOOKING ON THE BRIGHT SIDE

A few summers ago, I went to a family reunion weekend at a home in the mountains. It was lovingly planned to take advantage of the beautiful grounds and surrounding countryside, with activities including boating, fishing, golfing, and hiking, as well as barbecues, Family Olympics, and a night-time bonfire.

And then, of course, it rained for three days.

There we were on the first night, eighteen adult-sized people and six large dogs, sandwiched into one not-so-large living room. We immediately began to make the proverbial silk purse out of the wet sow's ear by figuring out how to get everybody laughing at once. One of the surest ways to do this is to show old home videos. Seeing everyone appear in their scrawny, scraggly younger incarnations, complete with stylish fashions and hair-dos, is always a very funny experience.

It turned out to be a great evening, and we vowed to make the best of whatever the weather brought us next. The sun did come out intermittently, but basically there was another day of dodging rain showers. The dogs had a grand old time, rolling in the freshly sprinkled grass seed on a lawn that had turned to mud and swimming in the not-so-clear (actually very brown) pond. In the midst of the weather changes, we had a water balloon fight, which made good sense, as everyone was getting wet anyway.

We were determined not to let the rain stop the program. The evening of the planned campfire sing-a-long, the chairs were carefully wiped and placed in a circle. We had two guitars playing old favorites, and we sang our way through two whole songs before the thunder rolled in, the skies opened up again, and we were chased into the house. But once back in the crowded and very damp living room, we kept singing and dancing, and somehow the never-ending rain just didn't matter.

We did manage to sneak in a softball game and a round of golf between the downpours, although it certainly wasn't the weekend that our hosts had envisioned. But what could have been a huge disappointment was, instead, treated as an opportunity to see how open and creative we all could be. We took some of the downtime to have easy, one-on-one conversations that might not have been possible if we had always been active. And by spending a bit of that time alone, we were able to enjoy quieter aspects of nature, such as the sight and sounds of deer running through the woods and the capture of a bucketful of tiny frogs.

Attitude can be everything.

✎ *Making Lemonade*
In your Notebook, take a page or two to reminisce about the times you were able to make lemonade out of your lemons.

FINDING YOUR HAPPINESS CONTINUUM

A few years ago, I went to a championship lacrosse game, my first in ages, and it was amazing. There's something about the energy of a large stadium, with so many people sharing the same experience at the same time; it's physical, it's emotional, and it's very, very powerful. A few days after the game, I spent the afternoon alone in my office. Outside, the sky was that luminous shade of blue you see after the rain has washed away all of the humidity. The air coming through the open patio door was soft and clean, the cicadas were just warming up for their summer-long chirping, and I felt totally at peace—two opposite ends of a continuum, each defining who I am, what I love, and what makes me happy.

When I look at what makes me feel good, I see a variety of things. They range from those people, places, and activities that soothe and comfort me to those that energize and excite. But it wasn't until recently that I became aware that these all exist on a continuum—my personal happiness continuum—and that knowing when and how to choose among the possibilities can make a critical difference in how well I function.

I used to believe that self-care was a reward that I earned for work well done and time profitably spent. You can probably guess, using those criteria, how often I rewarded myself. What that reasoning actually got me was constant pressure to get it all right, all the time, so I would "deserve" the pat on the back that I desperately needed to give myself.

It's easier to see in hindsight, of course, that I was perfectly emulating the legendary Greek ruler, Sisyphus, pushing that giant boulder up the hill, only to watch it always roll to the bottom again. It took time and more than a few illuminating moments to enable me to recognize the futility of continuing to do that.

I came to realize that my assumptions were creating the problem and that I needed to turn those assumptions upside down in order to change what wasn't working. So I said to myself, instead of putting self-care second, I would do just the reverse: assume that if I took good care of myself, I would be more likely to see work well done and time profitably spent.

What a difference! I could tell that I was on to something because I immediately felt that positive inner *ping* when my body lets me know that I'm moving in the right direction. So, in spite of protests from that pesky Inner Critic, I set about discovering what I could do for myself that would give me the sense of peace or energy that I require so I can do what I most need and want to do.

This was the fun part—making a list of everything that gives me pleasure (see Chapter Three). And as I compiled this list, I became aware of how different activities were grouping themselves into categories, according to whether they relaxed or energized me. They stretched out in a straight line from the calming influence of a meditative moment by my little fountain, to the euphoria of a last-second winning touchdown in a season-ending game. In between were items that produced simple comfort (such as wrapping myself in a warm towel, plucked out at the end of a dryer cycle) or a bit of stimulation (like dancing to a great but seldom-heard song on the radio).

What I had created for myself was a blueprint of how to bring me back to *me*. And it was naturally organized to promote whatever mood I wanted to experience more of. What this requires, however, is a sensitivity to where I am at the moment; I need to be conscious of how I feel in order to choose what would be most helpful. And that means there have to be "check-in" times.

At various points each day, it's important to check in with yourself to see how you're doing. It's so very easy to become distracted or overwhelmed and to be carried out with the tide without realizing what's happening. The key here is to be aware of how you feel, so you're in a position to make decisions about the use of your time that move you in the direction you need to go.

It can seem self-indulgent to focus so intently on what brings you happiness, but that's the root of what you send back into the world. Taking care of yourself—doing what you need to do to feel healthy and competent and spiritually nourished—provides the support for everything else you do.

✎ *What Makes Me Happy Revisited*
Go back to the "What Makes Me Happy" exercise in your notebook (Chapter Three). Recopy your list, grouping items according to whether they increase your sense of Calm, Comfort, Excitement, or Euphoria. Refer to each list when you want to experience more of that particular quality.!

ENJOYING PEAK EXPERIENCES

A few years ago, I had the opportunity to see a very special concert. The music was astonishing, the performances were brilliant, and the audience was moved to tears. The artist was Paul McCartney, and he took us on a forty-year journey through our shared past. It was a celebration of love and hope and perseverance over tragedy and loss. And I left there as impressed by the man's love of life and of performing as I already was with his musical genius.

What was especially impressive to me was watching an almost-sixty-year-old musician play with the same joy and passion he had shown as a twenty-three-year-old. A lifetime had intervened, but it hadn't left him tired or jaded. How many of us can say the same thing? And that was the most fascinating part of the evening. Yes, it was Paul up there on stage, but that concert was about us and what we've all been through in the years since we first came together in the early sixties.

Whether you're a Beatles fan or not, there's no doubt that their music served as a backdrop to coming of age in those times. (And by the way, it was almost surreal to listen to songs performed live that heretofore were limited to studio recordings.) The music, as always, brought back memories of how we were, who we were.

And that's what our most outstanding personal experiences do for us. They bring us to a peak of intense enjoyment that can be relived and remembered for as long as we're able.

One of my most memorable peak moments was the first time I ever galloped a horse across a beach—one of my lifelong dreams. A group of us were enjoying a quiet trek down a mountain in Saint Martin in the Virgin Islands. When we reached the bottom, we found ourselves in the woods at the edge of the sand, and suddenly my mare took off toward the ocean. She was determined but playful and, thankfully, stopped at the water's edge. Heart pounding, I slid off her back. I couldn't stop grinning; it had been even more thrilling than I imagined.

✎ *My Peak Experiences*
What have been some of your peak moments? List them in your notebook.

FINDING SERENITY

If enjoying your life at this moment means having more calmness than excitement, the good news is that you have more opportunity to create that calmness than you think you do. And you don't have to leave home to do it.

I won't tell you that all you have to do is think peaceful thoughts and you will feel serene, although I know that's an enticing concept. The real world is full of distractions and problems and pressure to get things done. Thinking peaceful thoughts can help, but it isn't the most comprehensive solution.

The bottom line, though, is that it is up to you to take yourself to your personal place of serenity, whether it's a physical location or exists only in your mind. How you get there can vary, but the decision to go is yours. What this means is that you first have to know what brings you peace—what thoughts, places, or activities quiet your mind and refresh your soul.

And then you have to make the choice to go. Too often, we believe that we have to wait for conditions to be just right before we're able to relax. Or we wait too long and wind up collapsing from exhaustion or the mental strain of trying to do it all. The choice to seek serenity is yours.

You start with the belief that it is your right to experience a certain amount of serenity in your life. You can't hear your gut—your intuition—unless you shut out your stressors for a while and focus on what you need to know, or do, in order to function in the most positive way possible. Calling a mental or physical time out is the only way to make it happen.

When you've made the commitment to care for yourself in the moment, you're ready to act: Can you get away? Can you be alone in your favorite room in the house? Can you go outside or to the gym? Can you possibly close your office door for a few minutes? Or perhaps all you can manage is to shut your eyes for a brief imaginary escape.

What you do next should reflect your personal style, that is, what typically works for you and what your needs are at that particular moment. Options range from deep breathing and meditation to tai chi or vigorous exercise. They can include sitting in absolute silence, listening to a fountain or soft music, focusing on a fish tank or a candle, or looking out the window. The goal is to bring you to a place where you feel calmer, more centered, more relaxed, and able to think more clearly. It's not so much what you do but where that activity or mental process takes you. If your stress is too great to manage alone, you may need to enlist the help of a friend or a professional for support in learning how to better care for yourself. But learning what to do and how to do it is essential.

Unfortunately, many of us subscribe to the belief that if we can just figure out how to do everything "right," our problems will disappear, and serenity will become our natural state because there will be little to disrupt it. Not so. Problems are life's ways of telling us what we need to work on, and what we need to work on changes as we move through our various ages and stages. The only thing we actually have control over is (ideally) our increasing knowledge of how to cope with what life throws us.

Being able to bring yourself to a place of serenity is a skill that you will use throughout your entire lifetime. The particulars may change, but once you've found your way there, you will be empowered to go there again and again.

BEING IN FLOW

The weather in my part of the world had been extraordinary. I never remembered a fall season this lovely. And it made me hear the call of the wild. In answer to this call, I got into my car and headed for—no, not the mountains. Or even the woods. I went to the county duck pond! Being a busy working mom in suburbia, this was the closest to nature I could arrange to visit in the little time I was able to get away. But what a getaway it was.

I first drove through there one morning after carpool, which was something I'd never done before. I just felt the urge to go. As I turned down the lane, I could see the pond in front of me, with steam rising off of it. I pulled into the parking lot facing the water and watched as the trees on the other side flamed magnificently in that early sun. It was so stunningly beautiful that I kicked myself for not bringing my camera.

Amazingly, the following morning dawned as clear and bright, and I headed back, this time with camera in tow. I couldn't stay long, but those few minutes framing shots through the viewfinder brought me such peace that I had to return.

And so it went, all week. I continued to drive through whenever I could, just to experience the pleasure of seeing such vivid colors under those cloudless blue skies. Then one day, I had an afternoon time window suddenly open up, and I immediately took off for the park. This time I got out of the car and walked to a nearby stream where I managed to find the perfect-sized rock to sit on. I sat there and just watched life flow by.

I saw a bright red leaf drifting past, and as my eyes followed it, I noticed the reflection of the colorful line of trees at the water's edge. I focused on that shimmer for a minute, and then my attention was grabbed by something moving beneath the surface. Beneath, above, beyond—so much gentle movement. I let myself get lost in it and entered that magical time and space dimension known as flow.

Flow is the state of being so much "at one" with whatever you're doing that nothing else exists; it's where you're totally present and conscious only of the absolute Now. Flow can be experienced spontaneously but usually requires some degree of attention. In other words, you create the set of circumstances that encourage flow to come about.

Chances are, had I not deliberately invited that moment into my day, I would not have been able to manifest the flow experience the way that I did. Had I walked to the stream with my mind full of to-do's for later that afternoon or allowed the sounds of distant trucks to enter my awareness, I could never have become part of the scenery, part of the moving stream.

But it's not necessary to get away in order to experience flow. All that's required is to let go. Be where you are and no place else. There's actually an incredible feeling of relief involved in choosing to do only what you're doing. Instead of experiencing the tension of your mind racing in several directions at once, you get to focus on the separate sensations of the immediate moment—what you're seeing, hearing, smelling, tasting, touching. And maybe, using the sixth sense, what you're intuiting.

Being in flow opens a doorway to your intuitive mind. By quieting everything down, you have a chance to hear what you normally can't through all the external and internal chatter. And you do need to hear this voice.

When you decide that you want to get to know someone better, you probably take the time to go to a local diner or coffee shop and spend an hour or two in private conversation. But have you ever thought of doing something similar with yourself? Do you look for ways to spend quiet time alone, exploring your thoughts and discovering how you really feel about things?

It's easy to be drawn to beautiful places when the season beckons. But our spirit calls to us all year long, and we can't afford to just wait for perfect days to respond. We can be in flow anytime—anytime we choose to enjoy being conscious, present, and totally in the moment.

PLAYING HOOKY

When you're caught up in the normal routine of busy life, it's easy to forget what your own thoughts sound like. So much of what we think and do is in response to what others think and do that it's easy to lose touch with our individual rhythms. And we often don't realize the extent of our "trained responsiveness" until we're not required to do it for a while.

That's why so many people go in to the office on Saturday mornings to get their work done. It's amazing what peaceful, uninterrupted time can produce. Obviously, we do need others in our personal and professional lives for a variety of reasons, but every now and then it's good to be able to stand aside and say, "This is who I am when I'm not required to be on call."

For instance, what time would you eat meals if you didn't have to get out the door at a certain hour, or if you didn't have a prescheduled lunch break or a regular family dinnertime? What time would you get up if your mornings were flexible? What time would you go to sleep if there were no household chores or no one else was controlling the TV remote? Again, there's nothing wrong with choosing to live your life in concert with the needs of others; what's important is not to lose touch with your own needs, desires, and preferences while you're doing it.

That's why I think there should be mandated Mental Health Days (or even weeks!)—days when you get to stay home by yourself, not because you're sick but because you're well and you want to stay that way—days when you can remain in your PJs the entire day if you want to, sleep in or be awake enough to welcome the dawn, watch dopey videos or read fabulous books, or eat ice cream for breakfast. And no one has to know. You get the idea.

Paradoxically, doing what feels good and right for ourselves is one of the best ways to care for others. When we're not running from pillar to post or overwhelmed with competing demands, we're in a much better position to be sensitive to the important people in our lives. And most of us do want to be sensitive. We want to have the time and energy to be the best kind of friend, partner, parent, manager, or employee we can be.

To do that, we need to be proactive. The advice given to people when they're about to work out is an example of being proactive: carry a water bottle with you and remember to drink from it regularly, *before you get thirsty*. If you wait until you're thirsty, it's already too late to keep your body as hydrated as it should be.

Playing hooky occasionally can therefore be very good for you. What's essential is to use the time to get back in sync with yourself, to refill the pitcher so that you're ready to face another round of daily living.

✎ *My Ideal Day Off*

In your notebook, describe your ideal day off. If you need to replenish your energy, check back to the "Drainers and Fillers" exercise in Chapter Three, and list some of the activities that fill you back up. Mark off a specific time in your calendar to engage in at least one of these activities.

COMFORTING OURSELVES

A friend and I were talking about comfort foods—the edibles that make you feel like you're five years old again, or any age when your problems could be solved or at least smoothed over for a bit by a bowl of something warm and creamy, lovingly served to you.

Oh, wouldn't it be nice if life were that simple—good food, no effort involved, no extra pounds? The important thing to remember now, though, is that we can take care of ourselves in loving ways without relying on grown-ups.

For instance, we can now read books without help. When's the last time you were alone with one of your favorites? Add a cup of your favorite tea, hot cocoa, or a cold lemonade on a summer's night, and you can block out your troubles for hours. Or how about a movie? These days, we barely have to wait past the release date for a new motion picture to be available right in our bedroom. Instant relaxation, inspiration, or laughter is ready for the choosing.

Planting a garden can be very therapeutic. (Did you ever ask your parents to send away for the seed packets advertised in comic books?) You don't have to know much more than you did back then to enjoy something easy, like colorful zinnias or sunflowers. And you can use a saw now, without waiting for your dad to come home and supervise you. You can actually plug in any power tools you want! You can burn CDs. You can even eat dessert *first*.

But with age, of course, comes responsibility. You are also now free to *over*indulge, and that can have serious consequences. So how do you give yourself the comfort of grilled cheese and tomato soup, when having grilled cheese and tomato soup is not in your best interests? The answer is that you need to find out what your mind, body, or spirit could really use—what grilled cheese and tomato soup actually represent to you? Caring? Acceptance? Love? What, exactly, would make you feel more whole?

Comfort has to do with replacing what's missing. When we're cold, it feels wonderful to sit in front of a crackling fire or snuggle into a quilt. When we're scared at night, we turn on all the lights. When we're lonely we call a friend. Eating, however, is a more complex response, because we eat for comfort as well as to satisfy hunger.

So, what is a reasonable replacement for a just-baked chocolate chip cookie? Sometimes there is none, but perhaps you could look around and see what you come up with—nothing too taxing, just an easy alternative activity to help yourself through the moment. Do you knit? Play the piano? Have a book of inspirational quotes to read? How about straightening up the floor of your closet or a corner of your office? Can you get out in the sunshine? Take a drive in the country and blast your favorite music out the window?

I enjoy looking at copies of old *Life* magazines. Starting with the forties and working my way into the present, I can remind myself that others have lived through more difficult times than I might be experiencing at the moment. It puts things into some sort of perspective. And I like to re-read old personal correspondence that becomes more and more precious over the years.

A client told me that she gets comfort from just wrapping her arms around herself. Hugging is very good. You can hug children (if they'll let you), pets, and stuffed animals. The sense of touch alone can be soothing. I have a blue bowl of polished stone chips on my desk that I can swirl my fingers through and relax into their delightful coolness.

✎ *What Comfort Means*
What does *comfort* mean to you? Write a page or two in your notebook.

GETTING OUTSIDE YOUR BOX

It's ridiculous how much pleasure I can get from small things, like hummingbirds, for example. I've always been fascinated by their odd little proportions, with their long beaks, tiny whirring wings, and seal-like bodies. I rarely saw them, however, until we decided to make an effort to attract more birds to our backyard this summer.

The funny thing about our "decision" is that we never realized one was available to us. For years I'd sit out on the patio, delighting in the arrival of each different species of bird, always hoping to see more. (The summer that my favorites, the cardinals, nested in our Rose of Sharon was the best ever.) But it was a passive enjoyment. For some reason, we never thought about being proactive and creating attractions that would bring in more birds to enjoy.

I'm not sure why, but one day I started obsessing about birdbaths and hummingbird feeders. We did some research on-line and interviewed our local flower nursery and bird store managers for ideas on creating a (very) small bird sanctuary.

The results, from my point of view, were spectacular. We built it and they came, and we've had a lovely couple of months watching adult birds and their babies, of all kinds, take advantage of our backyard amenities. So here's the question: What took us so long?

It certainly wasn't the time involved or the cost; those were minimal. I can't even say it was laziness; once we got the idea, we immediately took off. All I can figure is that we were stuck inside a box of our own making. Somehow we managed to sit out back all summer, every summer, saying, "Wouldn't it be nice to observe more birds? Wouldn't it be great to see hummingbirds up close?" and that would be it.

What does it take to move us in the direction of our daydreams and fantasies? Often, all we need is the realization that we can step out of our box. And it's quite an eye-opening experience when it occurs: "You mean I could have been having all this fun starting years ago?"

So how do we begin box hunting? How do we realize that we are capable of bringing more of the things we love into our lives? The first thing to do is to try to catch yourself when you hear words coming out of your mouth such as, "I wish . . ." or "Wouldn't it be nice . : ." Ask yourself, "What steps do I need to take to make that happen?" And if you hear yourself giving reasons why you couldn't do whatever it is, make a list of your obstacles and tackle them one at a time.

I once had a client who created a beautiful home office for himself in the finished basement of his house. He told me that he had problems with procrastination, especially when it came to administrative paperwork such as filing and forms processing. The truth was that he had procrastination problems when it came time to do *any* work that had to be done in his office. His preference was to work upstairs, where skylights provided much more natural light.

So, if he enjoyed working upstairs, what was he doing with a downstairs office? I asked him that question, and his response was one that I've heard many times before: "Well," he replied, "I figured that I should have privacy, and the basement was the most logical place to go." Logical, maybe, but hardly the right choice for a man who loved windows and light and natural views! Fortunately, we were able to switch his office locale with an upstairs guest bedroom, and the procrastination problem was solved.

An outside perspective can be helpful when identifying boxes. It was easy for me to see that my client's predicament came from his assumption that offices are supposed to be in "logical" places. But that assumption kept him trapped in a basement space that was all wrong for someone whose creativity flourished much more in the light of day.

The birds of summer are coming to my yard in greater numbers now because I wanted to see them, and I took action. Ask yourself what you're waiting or wanting to experience, and go after it. The smallest things can make the biggest difference in your life.

MAKING TO-DO LISTS FOR THE SPIRIT

This afternoon I was sitting at my desk, looking at my to-do lists. I have to-do's for my house, to-do's for my family, to-do's for my business. I have to-do's for the dog. But how many of them make me smile when I read them?

The answer is, "Too few." And that tells me that I'm out of balance. So it's time to create some to-do lists to raise my spirits!

✎ What Makes Me Smile

Take a sheet of $8^1/_2 \times 11$-inch paper and turn it horizontally. Make four columns, with the headings Just for Me, With My Partner (if you have one), With My Kids or Family Members, and With My Friends. And then start brainstorming about things you can do that make you feel good. Here's the only criterion: whatever you write has to make you smile.

Under "Just for Me" goes everything you keep saying you want to do when you get the time. It includes all possibilities, from long, steamy bubble baths, to an evening with the novel you bought six months ago, to a hike up the nearest mountain, to a class you'd like to take, to a recipe you want to try, or to a trip to a spa. Everything.

"With My Partner" is the column for planning enjoyable time with your significant other. This could also be wide-ranging, from having breakfast together to planning a cruise. Day trips into the city, tennis lessons, week-end getaways, DVDs to rent—plan something for just the two of you.

"With My Kids or Family Members" involves people you're related to and would like to spend more time with. Here is where you put ideas for events for the whole family to do together or with one or two others: taking your children out for a meal individually, so you can give them special attention, or inviting an aunt or uncle to join you; possibly you could plan a family reunion, a game of Monopoly, or a Sunday drive, or a trip to Disney World.

"With My Friends" identifies the people other than family members you would like more contact with. Can you plan an evening out with someone? A joint vacation? More frequent phone connections or e-mails? Meeting for coffee one day a week?

Now here is the critical point: *This list is just as important as your other to-do list.* Of course, many of us have been conditioned not to even think about this list until The Other One is completed, but you probably already know the truth about that myth. You will never, ever reach the bottom of your daily to-do list, and if you wait to take care of yourself until you do, you will be in quite a sorry state.

To feel balanced, you need to integrate the two lists, or at the very least pick one from each column of the second list to do each week. Because the truth is, it's generally not how busy we are that creates problems; it's what we're busy doing. When we feel out of balance, we start experiencing frustration or resentment, and only by giving attention to the things we miss can we start to feel whole again.

Let's make it even easier: What column in your life needs the most attention right now? Would you love more time alone? With your partner? More activities with your kids or parents or siblings? How about your friends? Whatever jumps out at you is where you should focus your attention first. Remember, it's not a question of whether you deserve the time to do these things. You don't "earn" time for fun. Taking care of your personal and social needs is a must, and it's what makes everything else doable.

I've found, though, that even when we make time to take care of ourselves, we're often quick to sacrifice it if someone else seems more needy. One way to keep a check on this tendency is to mark your "Time to Take Care of Me" hours with a yellow highlighter in your planner book or on your calendar. Call it your SunBeam Time. This is your special block of time, and every day that you give it up is a statement that the needs of others have taken precedence. Sometimes, of course, that becomes a necessity, but it shouldn't be the rule.

There will be periods of stress when certain things demand so much attention that balance isn't possible. But if you're aware of what's missing and what would make you feel better, you at least have the opportunity to fit in small activities wherever possible. It's your awareness that's so important here—the idea that you place both to-do lists side-by-side and make the time not only to pay your bills but to nourish your spirit.

✎ *My To-Do List for the Spirit*

Turn to a fresh page in your notebook, and create your own To-Do List for the Spirit.

REACHING NIRVANA

Nirvana—no, I don't mean the rock group. I mean the state of freedom from worry or pain that I achieved for a while on Monday, December 22, 2002.

It was a day like most any other day in early winter, brisk and bright. It would have been an exceptionally nice day from the start, except for three events: (1) our basement sewer line backed up, (2) my computer malfunctioned, and (3) I was informed that my signed publisher's contract had a crucial clause missing.

Ordinarily, any one of these occurrences would have been exasperating and all three together, maddening. But the oddest thing happened: I didn't get upset. Instead, I found myself in that wonderful, peaceful place that mystics have written about for millennia—that transcendent mountaintop where all is as it is, and "as it is" is fine.

I first realized that I wasn't in Kansas anymore when our representative from the drain-unclogging service arrived to snake out the backup. He was an affable kid but a bit clumsy. As he was maneuvering his equipment at the top of the basement stairs, he managed to unhook a framed picture from the wall, and it wound up perched on his back. He couldn't move without it falling to the floor, so I had to come back up the stairs and reach around and over him to lift the picture to safety. Ordinarily, I might have been a little annoyed at the vision of that picture possibly tumbling to the bottom of the stairs, but for some reason I was just amused.

I left him downstairs to begin work, and all went well until I heard him call for me. I knew he couldn't be finished yet, but I had a hard time keeping a straight face at what he told me next. Apparently, he had lost a crucial small tool and confessed that it had disappeared into thin air as he was holding it while simultaneously taking off his jacket. He said he didn't hear it hit the floor; it wasn't in his coat, and he couldn't figure out where it could possibly have gone. I asked him what it looked like—a straight silver rod with a hooked top—and for several minutes we both searched the area. Suddenly, I looked up at where my son's street hockey net was stored, and there was the tool, hanging delicately from the mesh.

I went back upstairs to my cold coffee, shaking my head at that little adventure, and noticed that I was smiling. Smiling? Yes, smiling at the absurdity of backed-up sewer drains and dropped pictures and disappearing plumbing tools.

So went the day, with tiny mishaps and larger ones. I had been having trouble with the computer; it was moving too slowly, given its cable connection. On AOL I couldn't even access the Internet anymore, and the guy who says "You've Got Mail" sounded like he was gargling. I bit the bullet and called for tech assistance, never an easy task with the big menu of options, transfers, and waits. But again, as I was navigating through the system and listening to the directions from the rep as to how to proceed, I found myself relaxed and open. Even when he talked to me as though I were an extremely slow child, I just chuckled.

My problem with the publishing contract was eventually resolved, too, and as I thought about the day I had to wonder who was inhabiting my body. After all, this was the beginning of a new week that had started out miserably, and I was sitting there feeling perfectly fine. And then it dawned on me.

This is what I had been reading about for so long. The state in which I found myself was a slice of nirvana—the condition of complete acceptance of "what is" without any attendant negative emotions, a place where one is totally in the present, dealing with whatever must be dealt with but from a vantage point of calm and ease.

My immediate reaction to this realization was, "I want to stay here! I want to live here!" It felt so delicious to "just be." Unfortunately, when I woke up on Tuesday, my problems had returned to their normal shapes and sizes. But not totally.

I had been to that mountaintop, and there is no forgetting what it felt like. It was a state of bliss that was remarkable for its unremarkableness, and I'm determined to go there again. I do know that approaching life the way that I have for the last ten years, positively and proactively, has had something to do with my receptivity. Maybe I wasn't ready to stay with that quantum leap, but having done it once, I'm going to do my best to head back.

When you can enjoy your life with its own special richness, it's time to turn your attention to giving back.

Give Back

Once we become who we are, where we are, and begin to enjoy our lives, we're in a much better position to give to others out of the overflowing fullness of our hearts. Making time to give back, in gratitude and appreciation for all that we've been allowed to enjoy, is the ultimate gift to our spirit because it permits us to use our special talents and abilities to enrich the spirit of others.

I believe that every one of us has a personal mission—a mission to contribute something positive through being who we are. Woodrow Wilson said, "You are not here merely to make a living. You are here to enable the world to live more amply, with greater vision, with a finer spirit of hope and achievement. You are here to enrich the world, and you impoverish yourself if you forget the errand."

You define your mission by expressing your interests and talents as completely as you can. Because you are unique, no one can make the exact same contribution that you can. If you do not have a mission or a purpose, your life will be about your problems. Once you have a purpose, everything else in your life becomes just something to handle.

According to George Bernard Shaw, "This is the true joy in life, the being used for a purpose recognized by yourself as a mighty one, the being a force of nature instead of a feverish, selfish little clod of ailments and grievances, complaining that the world will not devote itself to making you happy."

FEELING GRATITUDE

Recognizing that the glass is indeed half full rather than half empty is a powerful moment of truth. Do you recall the movie *Pollyanna?* Even if Disney is generally too saccharine for you, you still might remember the joyfulness of the scene in which Pollyanna takes glass crystals from various lamps in a house and suspends them in front of a bedroom window. Sunlight pours through the crystals and casts magical patterns on the walls and ceilings, thoroughly delighting a crabby old woman who's convinced that there's nothing to be either happy about or grateful for.

There are very simple pleasures to be enjoyed, if we're willing to look and to be a little creative. And there's a special lesson to be learned from crystal sun catchers, in particular. I have one in my office, and I've noticed that the most brilliant colors appear when the crystal revolves in the setting summer sun. There are colors present at other times of the year, of course, but they're not so bold. Sometimes I have to scan the walls very carefully to see them.

The sun, obviously, does shine brighter during certain times as opposed to others. Seasons come and go, as do good times and bad. Sometimes it's harder to see the light and appreciate the fact that it's still there, despite the dimness and cold.

I have a neighbor who, when she feels down, goes out and does a helpful turn for someone she knows who is less fortunate. She says doing that brings back her perspective and reinforces her awareness of what's positive in her life. Yes, sometimes you have to deliberately go looking for the colors.

Gratitude is what restores them to our awareness. Gratitude is realizing what we're lucky to have, be it large or small: our senses, a place to live, our health, family, friends, a cherished pet, a green thumb, a way with children, a special talent, a sense of humor, our integrity, coolness in the summer, warmth in the winter, and beauty anywhere around us.

Gratitude for what you do have, as opposed to misery over what you don't, is the centerpiece for giving back. It can be difficult to feel grateful when the sun doesn't ever seem to shine on you. But the wonderful thing about gratitude is that the moment you begin to experience it, you automatically feel lighter. Yes, it might be great to have all the things you really want to have, but true happiness resides in being grateful for what is already present.

✎ *What I'm Grateful For*
In your notebook, start a running list of things you are grateful for.

IT'S ALL IN THE DETAILS

Last Sunday, I had a wonderful afternoon meal at the home of my children's elderly godparents. It had been incredibly difficult to come up with a date that worked for all of us, and between the time we originally tried to set it up and the day we actually got there, we had several months of postponements.

Part of the problem from my end was that as we looked at each possible weekend, we had to contend with sports schedules, work schedules, study schedules, parties, and the inevitable winter illnesses. At times I thought, "We're just too busy to do this." And what a mistake it would have been to let that happen.

It's so easy to become habituated to the pace of our lives. We get used to the ever-increasing speed of things and think this is the way life has to be. But you may recall the story of the frog and the boiling water. If you put a frog into a pan of boiling water, it will, of course, jump out. The frog is not an idiot, and the water is too darn hot for it to stay in there. But if you put a frog into a pan of cool water and turn up the heat gradually, the frog will boil to death, because he gets used to the water becoming gradually hotter and isn't aware that he's getting cooked until it's too late.

There's a lesson here. Not until we get out of our pan for a minute do we realize what it's been costing us just to stay in that place. And only by taking some time away from our routine do we get in touch with what we've been missing. Yes, vacations and getaways are nice, but I'm not talking about those. I'm referring to simple breaks of just a few hours that restore our appreciation of the fundamentally good things in life.

My children's godparents are from an era when it was important to do things "right" when one is entertaining. Not for them the tossing of a few plates and knives and forks onto the table for a small luncheon. Oh no. We're always presented with a linen tablecloth and cloth napkins. There is a separate piece of silverware for every single course, and our name is written on the silver napkin rings. There are choices of little breads and crackers and cheeses, small plates of our favorite appetizers, and individual servings of water brought to the table in crystal bottles.

Everything was served that afternoon so carefully and lovingly that I found myself sighing and wondering once again, Why don't *I* make time to do things like this? And I'm not talking about Martha Stewart perfectionism. I'm referring to placing a value on slowing down to the point that, instead of patting myself on the back for how much I can do and how quickly I can get it all done, I pride myself on how I can make people feel the way my children's godparents make me feel.

The fact is, they did make me feel special that day. The *details* made me feel special. Looking around the dining table, I realized how easy it would have been to cut corners. Did they really have to put out two kinds of herring? Two separate main courses? Did they *need* to serve three different kinds of walnut-shaped cookies and two varieties of coffee cake? I mean—we're just family. Was it really necessary to pass out little towels for freshening our hands before dessert?

Of course not. And that's exactly my point. They didn't need to impress us. Everything was done the way it was done because it gave them pleasure to serve us with the same attention to detail that they would have given a visiting dignitary. We were of no less importance to them, and that fact was obvious and heartwarming.

Every detail of the table was a symbol to me of what I want my life to be about: the serving pieces that were collected from trips around the world, the curved salad plates that my daughter thinks are such fun to eat from, the individual cup of raw carrots that our hostess put in front of my son because she remembered how much he liked carrots. Each and every choice represented something of significance.

It's definitely possible to collect too much stuff in your life, so if you're going to be a caretaker of details, you want them to be the right details. It's important to be able to use or enjoy the things you have, or there's no point in having them take up space. Saving items that you love and sharing them with the people who matter to you should be what it's all about.

My dinner last Sunday brought me a fresh appreciation of several things, including the need to stop regularly and smell the coffee and to remember how important the small things are when it comes to letting people know that they're important to me. I'm going to make a renewed effort to remember this and hopefully not wind up like an overcooked frog.

✎ *What I Appreciate Most*
In your notebook, make a list of the small details around you that you appreciate.

APPRECIATING YOUR SUPPORTING CAST

I have trouble admitting that I can't be all things to all people all the time. I pride myself on how many folks I can hold up with one hand while juggling everything else I have to do with the other. But every so often, I get tripped up and discover (again) that I'm not superhuman after all.

At times, events are truly out of our control. And some things we cannot change or rush, no matter how much we want to. At these times, we have to rely not only on our ability to be patient but on the support of other people as well.

I read an article a few years ago about a famous actress and her thoughts on what made her successful. She was quite strong in her assertion that she could not have come as far as she had if not for the efforts of dozens of people. There was an accompanying photo of her on a huge lawn, surrounded by everyone she considered to be an essential part of her life, from best friends to her acting coach, psychotherapist, and even her dog's groomer. I was remembering this recently and wondering what my own "supporting cast" photo would look like today.

It would require a very large lawn, that's for sure. I never seem to realize how many people are behind me, caring for me and about me, until I stop and take a good look. Unfortunately, it seems to take a crisis to get me to take that look, and I know there's undoubtedly a better way to gain an appreciation for the size and makeup of my support network.

One way is to make a Mind Map of Support (see the next exercise). Mind mapping is a great tool for getting an overview of a situation—for seeing all the individual parts at once. What you do is take a large sheet of paper and draw a circle in the middle with your name in it. Draw spokes outward from that circle to other circles representing various areas of your life, such as your immediate family, neighborhood, organizations you belong to, workplace, school affiliations, and so on. And from each of those individual circles, create spokes for the name of every person you know you can turn to in time of need, whether the need has arisen yet or not.

I bet you'll be surprised by the number of spokes you have, especially those for people whose "help lines" you haven't yet activated. There are many people out there, in addition to those you frequently call, who have the wisdom, skills, and empathy to be on your team. You just have to recognize who they are.

My own supporting cast is quite diverse in terms of geographical location and personality. It even consists of people I haven't actually met in person yet! (In these days of instant computer connections, your network can be incredibly wide-ranging.) But I know, when the chips are down, where to turn.

So much has been said about the way we're all growing farther apart, about how we're becoming increasingly rude and insensitive to each other. Now that may be true at certain times and in certain ways, but my personal experience has been showing me the exact opposite. Perhaps there's something to be said here for getting what you expect to get.

I believe that people are fundamentally good and that they care. There are, of course, exceptions to that, but I still think our basic condition is a positive one—as we saw in the movie, *It's a Wonderful Life,* where George Bailey couldn't appreciate his own value until he saw it reflected in the out-pouring of love and generosity from the townsfolk of Bedford Falls.

There are times when each of us feels very alone, for whatever reason, and those are the times when we need to pull out our Mind Map of Support and remember those lines of caring and service. They exist, and they're there for a reason, many times because the connection exists both ways, that is, the people you turn to for support also turn to you. And if they don't, the support they provide to you enables you, in turn, to take care of others. It's a "system" set up for the benefit of all.

✎ *A Mind Map of Support*
In your notebook, create a Mind Map of Support for yourself.

APPRECIATING SERVICE WITH A SMILE

We recently bought a new car and were surprised and delighted by the level of service we received. I realize that it's not exactly a positive commentary on the state of sales-manship that I should be so blown away by the level of genuine warmth and professionalism there, but that's what happened.

I guess I've gotten used to the sad fact that the overall quality of service has declined since I was a kid; people just don't rush out to clean your car windshield the way they did in the fifties. That's not to say that certain individuals don't try to do their best. It's just that economics and the pace of living have had an impact on what we're conditioned to expect. So I'm always pleased when folks go above and beyond the customary and make my buying experience an event to remember.

It's amazing how powerful something as simple as a sincere smile can be, and it's not always the easiest thing to manage. I was once standing in line in a department store, waiting to purchase a few clothing items. The woman in front of me was either having a very bad day or was just not a pleasant person. She was impatient and quarrelsome, and the salesperson ringing up the sale was doing her best to be of assistance but having a difficult time of it. I was quite uncomfortable myself, having to stand there and witness the scene. When the customer finally left, the salesperson and I looked at each other and just shrugged. She thanked me for waiting, and I congratulated her on her composure. And then we laughed. I mean, what can you do?

To tell the truth, there are a number of things you can do to make already uncomfortable circumstances more comfortable. We've all seen situations in which people have lost their cool under pressure in long lines, in bad traffic, and in lousy weather. It can take a lot of effort to be part of the solution rather than part of the problem. But I give my heartfelt thanks to those who manage to do it. Whether you're a salesperson or a customer, an administrator or a patron, a medical professional or a patient, a business owner or an employee or a volunteer, patience and courtesy go a long, long way.

And that's why I always appreciate being treated well. Maybe I should be taking this for granted, but that's not reality. People do have good days and bad, and some, for whatever reason, just don't care. So when a person goes the extra mile for me, I remember it.

Effort and enthusiasm pay off. And so does good organization. When you are ushered through a system with crisp efficiency as well as friendliness, the results can be long-lasting. And there's that wonderful ripple effect: when you're treated with consideration and respect, you're much more likely to turn around and do the same for others.

So how come we're treated so well in certain places and not in others? I think it comes down to expectations. What are your expectations for the people who work for you? What about the people who live with you? What are your standards for how *you* are treated?

No matter how much progress we've made in the last few decades, no matter how far technology has brought us, manners still matter. I don't know about you, but I refuse to patronize places that don't make an effort to put forth their best. That's not to say that everything has to be perfect; I simply like to feel that my business and personal satisfaction are important to the people who are providing me service (and taking my money!).

And that goes for our home lives, too. Have you met the person, young or old, who doesn't relish being appreciated? When our efforts are noticed and valued, it's easier to feel good about what we're giving.

Never underestimate the value of giving and receiving with a smile. You never know how big a difference it can make in someone's day.

REDEVELOPING FRONTIER VALUES

There was a TV show on the Public Broadcasting System (PBS) a few seasons back called "Frontier House." Whether you watched it or not, you can appreciate two important concepts in the program that are still powerfully relevant today and worthy of discussion: *community* and *service*.

Community can be defined as "a group sharing common interests." I was fascinated by the dynamics of the family community depicted on the TV show and the way in which children understood their personal importance to their families. For instance, in the wilderness chores were not assigned so that children could earn their allowance. Instead, there was an obvious and direct link between performing one's chores successfully and the survival of one's family.

Compare this to the present day. I have come to realize that, unfortunately, my family will survive just fine if my children do not take out the recyclables and the garbage, wash the dishes, or feed the lizard and the dog. And why is this? It's because I will do it if they don't (bad idea). This strategy never would have worked on the frontier, because the parents would have dropped from exhaustion if they had taken on the physical responsibilities of their children in addition to their own. Unless everyone pulled his or her own weight, nobody made it out alive.

Day-to-day life in pioneer times was certainly not simple or easy. I'm very glad that I can provide for my children now without forcing them to work from dawn until dusk, and I'm happy that they have time to hang out and enjoy long conversations with their friends. Our lives are certainly easier than lives were back then. But the question is, Has our progress really been beneficial to everyone, or has there been a debilitating trade-off?

Today's kids don't get to see the relationship between what they do to help their family and the intrinsic value of that contribution. For example, if you went out and milked the family cow, you were able to put food on the family table. When you tended a garden, you did the same. If you built a drinking trough for the family horse, or put tar in the chinks of the log cabin roof, or sewed a dress, there was a visible connection between your efforts and the service that was provided.

And this brings us to the second concept: *service*. One of the definitions of *service* is "an act of helpful activity," but I don't believe that most of today's kids look at their family and household contributions this way. They give of their time because they hope to get something for it or because it's a mandate. They don't appreciate that they're part of a larger system in which the members depend on each other for a good quality of life.

The fact is, community and service go hand-in-hand. We build both structures and relationships through working together for the common good. So how do we get this family value back into our families?

Obviously, this is not a problem for everyone, and I applaud all those who've been able to instill an understanding of family community and service into their children. But many parents have belatedly discovered that their teenagers have grown up with an attitude of entitlement that is the polar opposite of what we were exposed to on "Frontier House." Watching "The Osbournes" today is to understand what parental largesse can create. Ozzy may mean well, but it's tough to rein in kids who've had the bit in their teeth for years.

So what can be done about it at this late date? I would like to see a return to the family community concept, and that means, once again, introducing children to their place of value within the home. For instance, I'm in favor of expanding the idea of the family meeting, which has become popular in the last few years, but I think we need to approach it a bit differently. Instead of starting in with family gripes and problems at the outset, the point should be made clear and in a positive way that every child is unique, as is every adult, and that everyone should be allowed and encouraged to contribute their special talents to the family.

Of course, there are still toilets to clean, floors to wash, dog and cat poop to pick up, and other less glamorous tasks that have to be assigned. But if we all learn, once again, how to rely on each other for the good of the whole and how to honor everyone's contribution, we will have far fewer burned-out parents and far more children with a well-developed sense of worth.

GIVING GIFTS

I enjoy the season of gift giving. I love looking through catalogues and boutiques and crafts fairs for the perfect present. Of course, perfection is a state of mind, but the fun for me is seeing how well I know my family and friends and how close I can come to giving them something they'd love to have but can't or won't buy for themselves.

Unfortunately, distance and years have interfered with the intimacy of some relationships, so a few years ago I sent out questionnaires asking for people's current favorites: music, authors, movies, hobbies, charities, sports teams, and so on. The respondents told me that they were pleased to be asked but were stumped for answers. Now, you know it can be hard enough to select the right gift for everyone, but how much harder is it when *they* don't even know what they like?

This is another reason to stay abreast of what delights you. Although some preferences will stay constant, others will come and go, and you'll miss the opportunity to take advantage of them if you aren't aware of what's going on in the "delight department" of your life.

We all know people who have collections, and that can make things easier for gift givers. For example, my daughter loves all things Kim Andersen (the children's photographer); my mom collects first-edition Kathleen Norris books, and my husband and I have a shelf filled with unique kinds of bells. Sometimes though, collections get to be too large or un-wieldy, and collectors have to say, "Enough!" My children's pediatrician amassed a huge number of stuffed frog gifts after he started wearing small ones attached to his stethoscope. It was the perfect conversation-starter with kids, until there was no space in his office that was free from frogs.

Often, one of the best gifts is the gift of time, especially for those folks who are either overwhelmed with demands or don't have the opportunity to get out much. Material items can be nice, but giving a coupon for free babysitting or reservations for dinner will be much appreciated by those who don't or won't take care of their own need for a break.

One mistake we need to watch out for is a tendency to present people with a gift that *we* think they should have. It's easy to be manipulative under the guise of holiday gift giving, but it's a very easy ploy to spot. Ask yourself, upon opening the present you selected, will there be a bigger smile on the face of the receiver or the giver? That should be your answer.

The art of gift giving lies in understanding that what's important in any exchange is the meaning behind it. Many of us can't afford extravagant presents, and therefore we shouldn't equate the level of caring with cost. And most of us don't have the time to design elaborate creations, either. What we can aim for, though, is to do what's sensible, with feeling.

I do suggest that you try to include a personal note with your gifts. Tell recipients what you especially appreciated about them in the past year and why you're grateful they are in your life. Long after the gifts have been put aside, your notes will remind others of what really matters to you, and the real gift is that you took the time to say so.

FINDING THE MEANING OF LIFE

In 1981, my dad suffered a massive heart attack. He was only fifty-eight at the time and was given 1-in-100 odds of survival. The doctors said that the critical factor would be his will to live, but we knew that might be a problem once he found out that he would no longer be able to run his retail shoe store, which had been the consuming focus of his life. Somehow, he made it through sixty-nine days in the hospital and was sent home depressed and still not knowing if he would be strong enough to get through the next several months.

As the weeks went by and his health improved enough for feelings of boredom to set in, I suggested that he keep a journal. He had always enjoyed writing, but I added a little twist. I gave him a pen with two colors, red and green, and told him to write in red ink when he felt down or angry and green when he felt more positive. Over the next six months, he wrote. In the beginning, his entries were mostly in red, but gradually the little oases of green grew and spread to the point where he could actually see himself getting better.

The last entry was made on the first day he was able to go out and eat at a restaurant. Today, he says, "Learning to live 'in a green state of mind' has made a powerful difference in my life. I now *look* for ways to feel good and know that when I do, I'm better able to deal with whatever's coming my way."

It was wonderful to watch the transformation in my father's outlook on life. In three years, he went from total self-absorption to displaying such community spirit that the county executive in Baltimore, Maryland, publicly recognized his volunteer efforts by naming a special day in his honor.

My dad made the choice to try out a completely different kind of life than he had lived before. You might say, "What choice did he have? He became disabled." But he could have made other choices. He could have ignored doctors' orders, gone back to his shoe store and had another, most likely fatal, heart attack. Or he could have stayed in the house, feeling angry or overwhelmed by the cards that had been dealt to him, and done nothing. But he made the decision to look at what he could do, given his limitations, and ended up helping himself by helping hundreds of others.

Life is so tenuous; it's not the best idea to go through your days looking over your shoulder, waiting for fate to catch up to you. Better to make the best of what you have, whether your life is to be the equivalent of a short story or a twenty-chapter novel.

And in addition to making it the best you can, I suggest that you leave something behind to shed light on your journey—stories and reminiscences that only you can share.

I will never know my great-grandparents, except through the shadowy memories of my parents. I look at the grainy old photographs and wonder who these people were and what it was like to come here from another country in the 1800s. In hopes of giving my children more solid remembrances of their own great-grandparents, I made audio recordings of them a few years before their deaths. The record was incomplete but nonetheless revealing. I was at least able to preserve the cadence of their voices—the sounds of laughing, singing, sighing. I only wish that I had been able to capture more of their thoughts.

Many people fear what others might think if they "really" knew who they were. But you know what? What we usually find out is that we're all up against the same kinds of things in life, and knowing that makes us all more human somehow. And it's the humanness that makes for the best memories.

Whatever you leave behind will be treasured by people who don't even know you yet. Anything in your words is better than nothing. I'm sure that anyone who has suddenly and unexpectedly lost someone can tell you this. And it's a gift to yourself as well. Writing about daily or weekly events or about first memories, steppingstones, or life turning points can bring about a certain kind of personal clarity that you may not be able to gain in any other way.

The total meaning of life—our own life—may be too broad to see in a single lifetime. But we can share what makes it meaningful to us and thereby keep that light burning for others.

SHARING OUR PASSIONS

The last time that I went to the dentist's office for a routine check-up, I came away with three things: clean teeth, a very good recipe for chicken parmesan pitas, and the address of a wolf preserve in a nearby county. (I came across the last two items while thumbing through a magazine in the waiting room, which just goes to show you that no time has to be totally wasted.)

Wolves have always fascinated me, but I've never been privileged to see them up close, so that's what I decided to do for Mother's Day. Yes, my family and I spent the morning at the Lakota Wolf Preserve. The preserve is small but well organized and allows you to observe four different wolf packs from a central observation area. Its tour guide is the seventy-year-old co-owner, Jim, who has spent the last two years creating a truly wonderful haven for the animals he loves so much. In Native American medicine lore, the wolf is a teacher—a pathfinder who returns to the clan to share knowledge and wisdom—and this belief is easy to understand when you look into those eyes; the fierce intelligence is breathtaking. But what actually impressed me most from this visit was Jim's story of how he had come to build such a place after a long career as a veterinarian and wildlife photographer. His was the story of one wolf and the care that it needed, and of Jim's journey to find a location where people could come to understand and appreciate the magnificence that he sees in these wild creatures.

It was his quiet passion that affected me so much. Laced with humor and with many facts about these seventeen wolves and wolves in general, Jim's talk was powerful because it was so genuine, not scripted or rehearsed or tired from too many repetitions. Jim is doing what he loves and doing it for a good cause, and I believe that this is the ultimate purpose in each of our lives.

Take a moment and reflect on the times in your life when you've been around people who had a real passion for what they did, whether it was their vocation or avocation, a full-fledged career, or volunteer job, or hobby. Do you recall how they looked when they spoke about what they loved? The sparkle in their eyes? The intensity of their energy? Can you remember what it felt like to be in their company?

I was channel surfing the other day and came across a cable show where a woman was taking viewers through her collection of antique pewter teapots. Now, I'm not very interested in old serving pieces, but I was intrigued by her enthusiasm for the history she discovered in each item and found myself listening to the stories of her findings as though I were an avid collector. It wasn't the teapots that fascinated me. It was her love of them that made her magnetic.

Most of us would say that our favorite teachers were those who shared their love of what they were teaching. It wasn't just that they made learning fun; it was as if, for a period of time, we were allowed to tap into what inspired their particular zest for life and become a part of it. I've experienced this with a summer camp counselor, a dog breeder, a linguistics professor in college, and a Broadway set designer, among others. And I believe that we all have this kind of magnetism within us.

We are drawn, individually, to whatever speaks to us, and our biggest gift to ourselves is to develop these talents and interests. Our gift to others, then, becomes the ability to simply share our pleasure in our interests or to take that pleasure further and help others awaken to their own abilities. And it's never too late to do this. One of my best friends has recently combined a talent for teaching with her passion for motorcycles and has become an excellent motorcycle safety instructor.

This takes commitment—a commitment to our own well-being and to the possibility of enriching others through the love of what we're doing. Let what you love become your contribution to the world.

✎ *Passionate People I Know*
In your notebook, make a list of people you've known or admired for their passions. How did they go about sharing those passions?

Were they teachers? Writers? How do you think that their sharing enhanced their own creative pleasure?

DEVELOPING MAGNIFICENT OBSESSIONS

I subscribe to *People* magazine, not so much for the celebri-
ty stories but for the features on "ordinary" folks who achieve
their fifteen minutes of fame through their interesting, unusual obsessions.

How is it, I wonder, that individuals come to be fixated
on Swiss cheese? Marbles? Recordings of everyday sounds?
Cookie jars? A recent *People* article about a man preoccupied
with the subject of extinct birds quoted him as saying, "You
don't choose your obsessions." But do you?

We're shaped by so many influences. Some of our obsessions are born of collectors' instincts; we want tangible evidence of the sights we've seen and the things we've done,
whether they be nostalgic memories or reminders of far-away
places. Maybe we've grown up around collectors or travelers.
Or perhaps we have to go farther back than that to discover
the roots of something that unaccountably drives our interests.

Since childhood, I have wanted to be a cowboy, which
has always made my parents scratch their heads. After all, I
was brought up in Average Suburbia, without role models for
this particular fascination. So where does this passion come
from? I used to be infatuated with TV westerns and riding
horses; somehow it all seemed familiar to me. But the only
answer that I could come up with was perhaps a past life
experience on the prairie.

Maybe that can explain my cowboy connection, but how do you make sense of a man's overwhelming zest for *mustard*—a zest so all-consuming that he opened a museum in order to display every different kind? (That, too, was in *People*.)

What I am most fascinated by are the special passions of individuals who are determined to make a difference in the world. I ask you: What makes someone campaign for cleaner water, as opposed to taking care of the homeless? Why are certain people drawn to raising guide dogs for the blind, while others fight to eradicate a specific disease? Some commitments can be linked to personal experience; others just seem to appear on their own.

What makes passions so personal? For instance, my son has been crazy about animals practically since he was born. Some of my earliest memories of him have to do with watching the Discovery Channel together on TV and being amazed at his level of concentration. As he grew older, he would reach out to any and all creatures that came near and seemed to have an uncanny ability to calm them. He has never doubted for a second that he would pursue a career that allows him to study and contribute to the well-being of wildlife in some way.

I wonder, how is it that some of us know our missions from the start, and the rest of us can take years to figure them out? Early in life, I knew that I loved to write. I composed poems and essays for school and thought I might become a professional writer. But when I was sixteen, I met a psychologist who inspired me to move in that direction. Now, years later, I appear to be circling around and developing one of my original passions. Only this time, I'm combining it with a particular sense of purpose: an intense desire to reach people through my writing in order to teach, encourage, and motivate.

Am I obsessed? Is my son? In a way, I suppose so. Everyone who fiercely loves what they do and believes that they're here on earth, in part, to do that, is in touch with their life force. It doesn't matter whether your force is your vocation, avocation, or just part of your role as a parent, partner, friend, or mentor. It doesn't matter whether you're here to educate or entertain, or to build or oversee what's already been built. If you can pass along some of your energy and dedication, you will have used your abilities well.

Should you find that your thoughts or emotions are dominated by something that spurs you in a positive direction, pay attention. It may seem out of character for you or even out of reach, but don't judge. Deep inside, we do know what's right for us. And what's right for us may be just what our own little world or the world at large needs to receive.

✎ *What Inspires Me*

In your notebook, describe what inspires you. Then think back to what you spent time doing as a child. Do you see any connections? Ask yourself, If I could take a year off work to do *anything*, what would it be? Is there anything I've dreamt of doing? Is there a contribution I'd most like to be known for?

BEING PRESENT IN SOMEONE'S LIFE

Sometimes your contribution is made so quietly that you never even know its impact . . .

I sat at the glass table I use for a desk, looking through the open patio doors. Fifty yards away was the wooden deck of a house, wet and empty on that Thursday afternoon: no children bouncing up and down the stairs on their pogo sticks; no Zoe, the Portuguese water dog, bounding around them in circles; no parents, cell phones clamped to their ears, wandering in and out of the open doors, keeping an eye on the action.

They had moved to the other side of town. I knew nothing of the move until the morning the truck pulled up to their house and only found out later from another neighbor where they had gone. I didn't know them at all except for the occasional acknowledging wave, yet during the last six years every one of them had somehow become a comfortable, reassuring part of my world. I really missed their presence.

I'd been puzzling over this for days. How could I feel this way about people whose names I never even learned? I don't have answers, but my feelings tell me that something about their lives or their lifestyle touched me very deeply.

When they first moved here, the family consisted of a mother and father in their thirties, with three children—two girls and a boy. And a puppy. The youngest child was about two and the oldest eight. The house had originally been a rental property, and when they purchased it, it was rundown. Over that first year, they did a lot of yard cleanup, removing unhealthy trees and bushes and vines that had taken over the house. The end result was that I could actually see the place for the first time.

With my office facing the back of their house, I now had a nice view whenever I lifted my head from my work. Over time, I unconsciously got into the rhythm of their routines. For instance, I always knew when spring had unofficially arrived, because they would begin opening the double doors onto the deck. I figured they must not mind the occasional fly or bee or mosquito because they didn't install screen doors. And it was a bonus that everyone could move in and out without the additional squeal or slam of a screen.

They hung lovely flower boxes and put large pots of colorful, seasonal blooms on the steps of the deck. They dug a vegetable garden against one brick wall and planted everything from tomatoes and squash to little autumn gourds. And I could almost set my watch to the hour when the woman would return from a day's work and come out back with her silver watering can or sprayer.

There were birthday parties and evening barbecues on the tiny lawn, and Sunday morning coffees on the deck, along with late outdoor lunches following a swim at the neighborhood pool. I could see when the kids had playdates, when out-of-town relatives were visiting, and when close friends would just hang out together in the candlelit darkness. I would experience the sadness that came as the double doors were closed and locked against the coming winter.

We were in such close proximity, you would have thought all that activity would produce a lot of irritating noise. And yes, there was noise, but it was not irritating. That was the amazing thing—there was always laughter coming from that house. Friends and family shared times together that were clearly enjoyable. And as that positive energy rippled out in my direction, I felt like a de facto family member at their get-togethers.

That's not to say that they didn't have problems, as every family does. There were evenings when one of the kids would stomp outside and sullenly kick at something imaginary on the deck, or when the husband would be out working on a project and his wife would come out with her arms tightly crossed and start talking to him intensely. But those were rare moments, and my reminiscences now are of the pleasant and fun days that one family spent together, which is way too uncommon these days.

My life has changed greatly in the intervening years, and in some ways it's hard to believe that I'm the same person I was when they moved here. As I watched those children get older and Zoe the dog get larger, I was able to sense that my own growth was keeping pace, and maybe that's what made me feel so much a part of the process.

Time definitely marches on. A new family has moved in, but they don't seem to like the out-of-doors as much. So I'd like to say to The Neighbors I Never Knew, wherever you are: "Thanks for the memories."

Sometimes "giving back" means just to be *present* in someone else's life. Never discount the value of a single human being to make a difference: *you*.

CONCLUSION

The End of One Story

A man of ritual, routine, and regularity, my father opened my biweekly e-mail newsletters at precisely 11 o'clock on Saturday mornings. It didn't matter that he had been up since 5:00 or that I usually sent them before 10:00; his time to check his mail was 11:00. Period.

My dad passed away suddenly on May 7, 2003. Fortunately, I was with him, in town to help my folks out after my mother's mild stroke three weeks previous. Even though he had survived a massive heart attack twenty-two years before and four subsequent cardiac arrests, it came as a shock that it was finally his time to go.

As I contemplated writing my next newsletter, I didn't know how to deal with the fact that my father wouldn't be sitting at his computer, ready to read it, ever again. But a wise friend told me to write it anyway, because my dad would still receive it—he would simply be at another address.

My dad was a complex and stubborn man, and that's probably what kept him alive for so many extra years. He insisted on things being done his way, and only his way, but after his attack he left an impressive legacy of public service through his twenty-two years of volunteer work for many organizations.

The night before his funeral, I lay awake, wondering what exactly I could contribute for my part of the eulogy. My husband told me not to worry, that somehow my dad would "tell" me what to say. The next morning, my mother came to me with an envelope that she had taken from the back of her desk drawer. It read, "To Be Opened Upon My Demise" and was signed by my father. "I knew this was there," she told me, "but I have no idea when he wrote it." We opened the envelope, which contained one sheet of paper, with but a single sentence written on it, summing up what he believed to be the purpose of his life.

As my father demonstrated to me, "Organizing for the Spirit" means to become who you really are—to discover what makes you unique and personally powerful so that you can experience the joy of living and of sharing your gifts with others. Organizing for the Spirit is a lifelong process of discovery and self-development, and the ultimate personal adventure. As my dad wrote in his final message: "To leave the world a bit better—to know that a life has been changed because you were there—this is to have succeeded."

Whatever your own definition of success, *Organizing for the Spirit* provides the foundation and roadmap for finding your way. Keep your notebook handy and continue to ask the questions. Listen for the answers.

It's never too late to become who you are meant to be.

The Author

Sunny Schlenger is the author of the best-selling *How to Be Organized in Spite of Yourself* (Penguin-Putnam, 1999). She is an internationally recognized professional organizer and coach who has helped thousands to master the dual challenges of staying productive and feeling good. She is also the CEO of SunCoach, Inc. (http://www.SunCoach.com), whose services include consulting, training, and public speaking. Sunny is currently producing a workbook for *Organizing for the Spirit*.